ARTIFICIAL INTELLIGENCE IN EDUCATION

A Non-Technical Look At The Future Of Education

Constantine Leo Serafim

Artificial Intelligence in Education

Copyright © 2024 by Constantine Leo Serafim

All rights reserved. No part of this book may be reproduced, distributed, or transmitted in any form or by any means, including photocopying, recording, or other electronic or mechanical methods, without the prior written permission of the publisher, except in the case of brief quotations embodied in critical reviews and specific other non-commercial uses permitted by copyright law.

For information contact: constantine@serafim.me

ISBN : 9798322597711

Book 1, First Edition: 2024

DEDICATION

This book is a tribute to the pioneers at the intersection of technology the visionary technologists who dream of a world where learning knows no bounds. Their dedication and vision have paved the way for this exploration into the realm where artificial intelligence enhances the human quest for knowledge. Also, to the tireless educators and curious students, this book is a testament to your unwavering commitment. You are not just recipients of this revolution but integral to it. May this work illuminate the path towards a future where artificial intelligence and human wisdom unite to unlock the full potential of every learner's journey.

Together, we chart the course towards a horizon where every mind finds its light, guided by the insights and innovations shared in this book. This is a collaborative journey, and your participation is crucial.

With profound gratitude,

Constantine Leo Serafim MBCS

Table of Contents

Introduction to AI in Education 1
- *The Role of AI in Early Childhood Education* 4
- *Leveraging AI for Enhancing Education for Individuals with Dyslexia and ADHD* 10
- *The Evolution of AI in Modern Education* 17
- *Basic Concepts of AI: Machine Learning, Natural Language Processing* .19
- *The Benefits of AI in Education* 22

Trends in AI-Enhanced Education 26
- *Adaptive Learning Technologies* 29
- *Reflecting on Improvements for Adaptive Learning Technologies* 40
- *AI-Driven Analytics in Student Performance* 43
- *The Significance of AI in Modern Education* 43
- *Automated Grading and Feedback Systems* 52
- *AI in Curriculum Development* 60
- *Examples of AI-Driven Curriculum Development* 63
- *The Impact of AI-Driven Curriculum on Teacher Roles* 65
- *Challenges and Ethical Considerations of AI in Curriculum Development* 70
- *Integration of AI-Driven Curriculum in Non-Traditional Educational Settings* 72
- *AI in Educational Assessment* 75
- *AI's Impact on Special Education* 78
- *AI's Role in Teacher Professional Development* 81

Challenges of Integrating AI in Education 84
- *The Impact of AI on Educational Policy* 87
- *The Digital Divide and Equity Access in AI in Education* 90
- *Teacher and Student Adaptability to AI Tools* 93
- *Data Security and Management* 96

Prospects of AI in Education and Personalised Paths 99

Enhancing Student Engagement Through AI 102

The Future of Teacher Roles and AI Collaboration 105

AI as a Collaborative Tool 113

Scaling Quality Education through AI 116

Integrating Graphical Analysis, Generation, Image Classification, and Object Detection in Education 122

Deepening Understanding with Advanced Visualization 126

AI Technologies and Chatbots in Education **129**

Virtual Reality (VR) and Augmented Reality (AR) in Education 144

Blockchain for Secure Educational Records 164

Predictive Analytics in Student Success 173

Exploring the Horizon: Role of AI in Enhancing Language Teaching and Learning Methodologies. **177**

Case Studies: AI Applications in Education **187**

Duolingo - Revolutionizing Language Learning Through AI 187

Implementing Adaptive Learning in STEM Education 188

AI-powered Educational Games and Simulations 193

Training Programs for Teachers on AI Tools 196

Policy Frameworks for AI in Education 199

Fostering a Culture of Innovation and Continuous Learning 201

Global Perspectives of AI in Education **208**

Comparative Analysis of AI Adoption in Education Across Different Countries 208

Success Stories and Lessons Learned 212

International Collaboration and Policy Development 214

Ethical and Social Implications of AI in Education **220**

Addressing Bias in AI Algorithms 226

Social Responsibility and AI 233

Creating Inclusive Educational Environments with AI 236

Ethical, Explainable and Responsible AGI in Education 240

Future Directions for AI in Education **247**

Emerging AI Technologies and Their Potential Impact 250
Navigating the Future: AI Challenges in Education and Strategies for Success 258
Vision for a Globally Connected AI-Enhanced Education System 261

How AI is Transforming Education Across the Globe 268
The Global Renaissance: AI's Transformation of Education 270

FOREWORD

In an era where technology reshapes our lives at an unprecedented pace, the fusion of artificial intelligence (AI) with education represents not just a frontier of innovation but a promise of a more personalised, accessible, and profound learning experience for individuals across the globe. This book explores that promise, a deep dive into how AI can transform educational landscapes, making learning more engaging, inclusive, and effective.

The journey of AI in education is a testament to human ingenuity and our relentless pursuit of knowledge. From intelligent tutoring systems that provide personalised feedback to students to data-driven insights that enable educators to enhance their teaching strategies, AI is not just a tool but a partner in the educational process. It offers a lens through which we can reimagine what it means to learn, teach, and grow.

However, with great power comes great responsibility. This book delves into the ethical considerations, challenges, and opportunities when integrating AI into education. It is a narrative that balances optimism with caution and innovation with ethics. It explores how we can harness AI to enrich education while ensuring it serves learners' diverse needs and values worldwide.

The authors bring together perspectives from educators, technologists, policymakers, and students, weaving a comprehensive picture of the current state of AI in education and its potential future. Through case studies, research findings, and visionary insights, this book aims to equip readers with a nuanced understanding of how AI can enhance the educational experience, making it more personalised, accessible, and effective for learners everywhere.

As we stand on the brink of a new era in education, this book is more than an invitation. It's a rallying call to dream, debate, and deliberate on the role of AI in shaping the future of learning. It's a call to action for educators, technologists, and policymakers to come together, collaborate, and create educational environments that leverage the best of what AI has to offer. Together, we can pave the way for a future where everyone has the opportunity to reach their full potential.

Welcome to the conversation. Welcome to the future of education.

CHAPTER 1

Introduction to AI in Education

The advent of Artificial Intelligence (AI) in education is not just a change but a transformation. It heralds a new era of redefined teaching and learning processes, promising to reshape educational paradigms for students and education providers. This introduction explores the use of AI in education, diving into the concept, its applications, benefits, and challenges that transform the traditional educational ecosystem. The next inevitable step is the evolution of AI technologies, leading to further advancements in the educational system. This is an entirely new era for academic settings, where learning is personalised regarding efficiency and accessibility, with new considerations and ethical implications.

AI in education is a cluster of machine learning algorithms, natural language processing, and data analytics used to develop intelligent, individualised, and automatic educational tools and systems. The first one has AI-powered technologies, which enhance student learning experiences and help academicians deliver effective teaching by systemising activities regarding administration in universities.

Artificial intelligence (AI) in education disrupts the old way of teaching and learning. The spectrum of features within education AI, from personalised learning algorithms to administrative automation, dramatically changes how educational content is delivered, perceived, and coped with. This book, therefore, attempts to explain further the role of AI in education, its applicability, and any challenges that may be experienced, thereby allowing us to anticipate what the future holds for this burgeoning field.

Figure 1 Here's a realistic view of AI in education, capturing the seamless blend of technology and learning in a futuristic classroom setting.

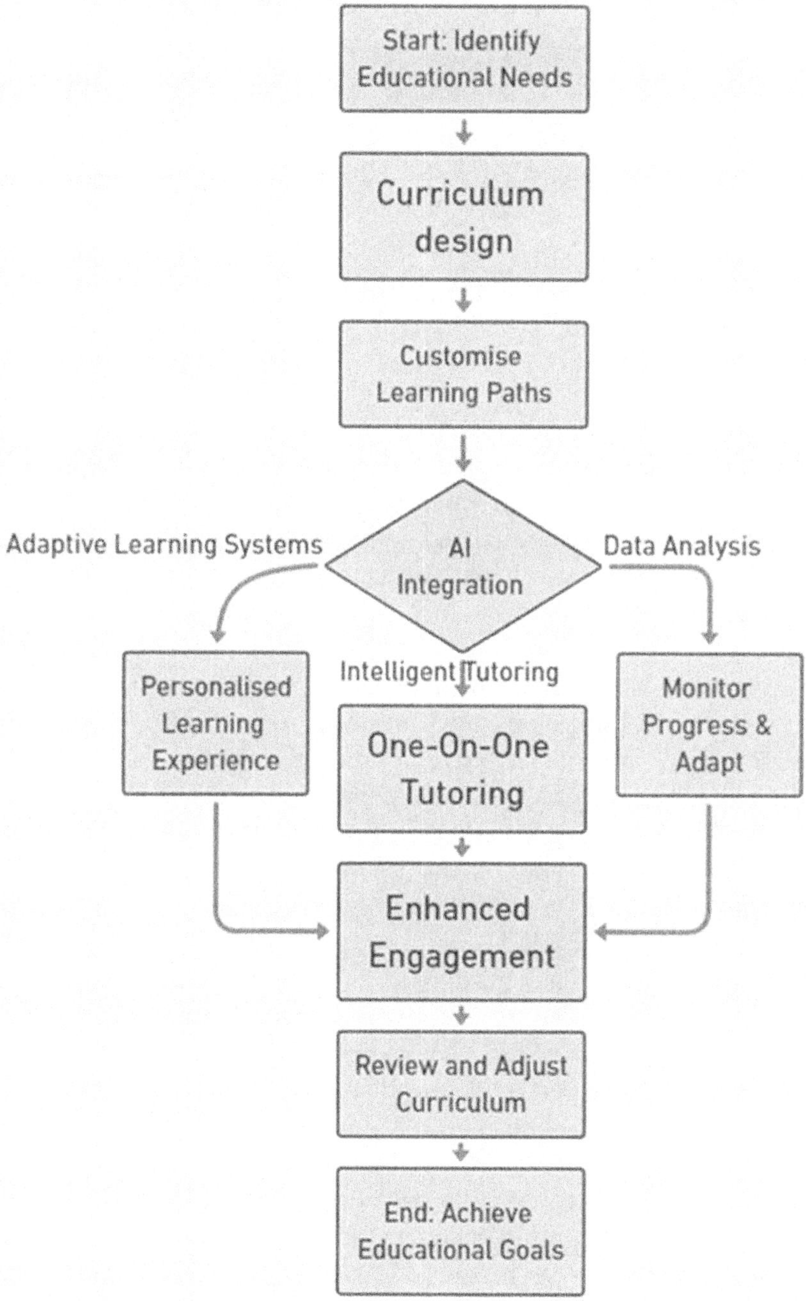

3 | ARTIFICIAL INTELLIGENCE in Education

Figure 2: AI in Education

The Role of AI in Early Childhood Education

Artificial Intelligence (AI) is said to have changed the world within various sectors, and education has not been left behind. Within the scope of early childhood education, AI may change the learning experience for little children. In the educator's and teachers' domain, some personalised learning experiences, improved assessment and grading systems, improved design and development of curriculums, and support systems in unique needs education may be devised through AI technology.

The use of AI in early childhood education has one major strength: it provides personalised learning experiences for students. AI-driven systems for personalised learning support a child's style, pace, and preferences needed to reach their potential. This individualised approach can help educators identify strengths and weaknesses, resulting in more focused support and interventions.

AI can also streamline the educator's evaluation and grading through the in-built assessment system. AI could bring valuable insights into student performance and their journey through the data collected from quizzes, assignments, or student interactions. So, this is entirely a data-driven position that can, as a result, inform the educator about areas in which learners are supposed to experience some difficulties, enabling the teacher to give.

Additionally, AI can produce better curriculum design and development by scouring massive educational data sets to find trends and patterns. Thus, educators can design, develop, and even modify more perfect learning resources that fit and motivate students' interests and needs.

In this regard, AI would offer novel solutions to individually aid each student, targeting their diverse learning needs within special needs education. In such cases, AI solutions greatly help special education-requiring students, as they offer everything from personalised learning experiences to adaptive assessments and even assistive technologies aimed at helping these students manoeuvre their barriers.

In a nutshell, it can be concluded that AI is expected to transform how early childhood education happens, with its excellent tools to improve early childhood educators' teaching and learning experience. Suppose educators harness the potential of this AI technology. In that case, they are in a position to design learning contexts for young children that would be more interesting, individualised, and effective in application.

The first years of a child's life are crucial for all cognitive, social, and emotional development trajectories. Early childhood education provides a base where all these development trajectories combine and set a tendency for future behaviours. With relatively fast strides in artificial intelligence, many opportunities are opened to enhance these first educational experiences.

AI opens the door to new kinds of personalised learning, which, with intelligent support, enhances both young pupils and educators or, generally, learners. This book looks at AI's role in early childhood education and how transformational it will be in allowing for benefits and new perspectives to educational methodologies.

Personalization of Learning

The traditional approach of one-size-fits-all in modern early childhood education must be updated. AI is at the forefront, giving tailor-made learning experiences that are bound to be changed according to the desired speed and set pace of young kids, for example, in analysing the interactions and progress of a child on an adaptive learning platform by personalising the educational content for them in style and pace of learning.

This, therefore, means that such customisation assures the early learners of practical and fun learning since they will be getting support and needs to be catered to.

Engagement and Interactivity
AI will be at the heart of early childhood education, propelling a more engaging and interactive approach to the field. AI will come with games, stories, and learning apps that are presumed to make learning the world of information more engaging and fun.

• **AI-Driven Educational Games:** These games, empowered by artificial intelligence, adapt the challenge of a puzzle to the learning stage of a child, hence making more sophisticated abstract ideas easy to learn and fun to realise. They generally engage their users in elementary arithmetic, languages, and problem-solving activities, making them develop the required skills in an engaging and fanciful environment that thrills them into wanting to play the game.

Interactive learning tools: Besides the games, AI has developed interactive learning tools that provoke an environment of exploration and creativity. For example, AI-based interactive drawing tools could give instant feedback and help build the kids' inner creativity; otherwise, it would remain hidden. Such is the case for storytelling apps that use AI technology to adapt the stories as per a child's response; hence, each story is an independent, interactive adventure that deepens comprehension and vocabulary for the given answer by the child.

Social and emotional development: Interactive AI tools support children in learning and developing holistically. The development of children through the activities facilitated by AI emphasises building their ability to think critically and solve problems. Most AI applications are group-oriented to help in the learning process for young learners, such as AI's use in group collaboration that fosters sociable interaction and children's activities.

These AI tools are interactive and exciting. They offer a whole new definition of early childhood education and move it away from the dynamic learning surroundings of today. AI enables educators to create an instructive and profoundly engaging environment, laying the most robust possible basis for lifelong learning.

Early Detection and Support for Learning Disabilities

The promise of Artificial Intelligence in transforming early detection and intervention for children with learning disabilities is bright. AI's analytic power can allow educators and parents to intervene much earlier in a child's life by providing focused support that will dramatically change educational outcomes.

Learning Disability Diagnosis: Diagnosis, either human or AI system-based, examines patterns in the child's behaviour and learning progression that may indicate or suggest the emergence of a learning disorder, such as dyslexia or ADHD. These systems can detect subtle signs often overlooked in traditional educational settings, enabling early diagnosis. Early identification is essential during this period since specific educational strategies and interventions can be provided to assist in facilitating the possible negative impact of these disabilities on the child's learning trajectory.

Personalised Interventions and Support: Identifying a probable learning disability makes AI-supported platforms increasingly essential to help develop a customised learning plan for the child according to his needs. This could be attributed to the fact that the websites could be set at the task's difficulty level, allow more practice of certain concepts that pose difficulty, and present the instruction in an alternative way that will be more akin to the child's learning style.

This ensures that support is accorded to children with learning disabilities so that they can succeed intellectually within the school environment.

***Supportive for Teachers and Parents*:** The AI tools support the children, and thus, they offer much-needed support for teachers and parents.

AI tools can help educators learn about different interventions and effective teaching strategies for students with learning disabilities. AI-driven applications and tools may also assist parents in guiding their children to learn at home, thus consolidating the school's different education interventions.

Such integration of AI into this early diagnosis for the support of learning disabilities would, Therefore, be a giant step toward ensuring that every child, irrespective of the magnitude of their learning challenge, gets proper support from inception. Such would be enabled through improved learning experiences since the capabilities of AI can be capitalised on to make early childhood education more inclusive, supportive, and effective for every learner.

Educational Content Creation and Curation

The capability of AI to develop and curate educational content in the context of early childhood education grants changeable and responsive competence that has the power to change as its young learners' changing needs require. This will ensure that all the stuff presented is within the correct age range and aligned to progress in learning and children's interests, which depends on.

Age readiness of content: AI can scan a great variety of educational material and reveal details necessary for developing or suggesting content that would be the most relevant to a child concerning age, level of learning, and interest. Creating personalised content ensures that young students are well-rested with meagre tasks or exposed to advanced content; instead, they can focus on their studies with just the right motivation.

Dynamically Adjust Content in line with Learning Progression: The AI system will be able to continuously monitor children's learning interactions and progression and hence keep changing the complexity and modality of educational content on the fly. For example, if the child quickly masters counting numbers, AI could help ensure the learner is not bored by the exercise by introducing even higher-level math concepts or problems. Where the child finds it hard to understand a given topic, on the other hand, the same topic will have more exercises to help in its comprehension.

Supporting Varied Learning Styles: AI content curation extends to academic subjects but includes many learning styles and methods. For example, some children prefer learning better through visualisation or audio guidance, while others prefer hands-on activities. In that case, AI can curate content according to such preferences for a better learning style and outcome.

This approach to content creation and curation departs from static textbooks and one-dimensional, tedious teaching methodologies, allowing for an engaging, adaptive education world that is personalised and caters to the needs of every young learner at the required level.

Integrating AI in early childhood education is a revolutionary way through which educational content reaches a learner and gets experienced. AI sets the stage for a future in which personalisation of learning, enhancement of engagement, support for early detection of learning disabilities, and dynamic development and curation of educational content could allow each child to fulfil their full potential from the very earliest stages of education.

As we look to the future, the role of AI in early childhood education will undoubtedly continue to evolve and expand. Modern AI, implemented properly with ethics and human oversight, will be able to improve upon the traditional modes of teaching by providing the next generation with a rich, adaptive, and inclusive learning environment.

The promise of AI in education lies not in the power of technology but in enabling every young learner to fulfil their unique talent and ability, helping establish a strong foundation for lifelong learning and success.

Leveraging AI for Enhancing Education for Individuals with Dyslexia and ADHD

Artificial Intelligence (AI) is an unbelievable concept in tailored education, providing out-of-the-box solutions for the disparate needs of students, including those with dyslexia and ADHD. Traditional settings in the learning space pose many challenges for a person with dyslexia and ADHD to thrive. This book discusses how the technologies of AI work towards filling those voids and offer "inclusive and supported educational experiences" for all students.

Understanding Dyslexia and ADHD in Educational Contexts

Dyslexia is a common learning difficulty that predominantly impacts the individual's literacy skills in reading and writing. These skills are often scattered with problems related to phonological processing, spelling, or automatic word recognition. Conversely, ADHD impairs the learner's attention, impulse, and organisational skills, making it very difficult for them to cope with the typical classroom environment. Therefore, innovative educational approaches are needed to support each student's unique learning styles and needs.

Such disorders, which make learning and classroom behaviour difficult, are dyslexia and ADHD, both widespread neurodevelopmental problems. The latter is a point that requires educators and parents to develop education in more tailor-made ways with respect.

Dyslexia is a difficulty characterised by problems in word accuracy or fluency, poor spelling, and decoding abilities.

Usually, these difficulties do not result from a deficit in cognitive abilities but arise from the phonological component of language. It's more than just jumbled letters; dyslexia affects how the brain processes written and spoken language. Students with dyslexia may take much longer than their classmates to read text or instructions and be hopeless at conventional reading and writing activities at school.

They may need help with a proper sequence of information, which can affect comprehension and, more significantly, the assimilation of classwork. However, in the face of all this, it remains essential to understand that dyslexia does not affect intelligence. Most dyslexics are said to be highly creative, and many excel in fields that do not require much reading and writing.

Attention deficit hyperactivity disorder (ADHD) primarily affects attention impulse control and executive functions. In the course of such conditions, students with ADHD may find it hard to concentrate on the task in question, be able to follow detailed instructions, or even work with timescales. Impulsive actions may also take place, which can disrupt the class.

Educational settings using the traditional pedagogical approach, which requires long periods of focused attention or silent sitting, may prove difficult for learners with ADHD. However, they tend to perform well in interactive and stimulating environments where lessons are short. Still, they are divided into shorter, digestible chunks with lots of scope for movement and physical activity.

In addition, the overlap of dyslexia and ADHD further complicates this. Studies have indicated huge overlaps between the two areas, with many students showing double conditions. Such an overlap may cause more severe problems with learning, but it shows that teaching needs to be multidimensional, which can precisely target students facing double conditions.

The educational implications, of course, can genuinely crystallise: one size doesn't fit all. Effective learning environments are pivotal with a firm understanding of the particular needs and strengths that learners with dyslexia and ADHD bring to the picture.

This includes using multisensory teaching approaches, using technology, and a supportive classroom environment that is understanding. Assistance to target recognition of potential and appropriate intervention will likely enable these students to break the barrier and realise their full potential in academics and creativity.

The Role of AI in Supporting Dyslexia and ADHD

AI-Powered Learning Tools AI-driven learning tools are built so learners can learn at their own pace and in the best style. Students with dyslexia can have the support of reading AI that offers on-demand reading assistance, points out phonetic patterns, and even recommends better learning strategies.

AI-based applications give students with ADHD a structured and stepwise learning process, which contains information on how to keep attention and distribute efforts properly to cope with the task effectively.

Speech Recognition and Text-to-Speech

Speech recognition and text-to-speech technology can benefit students with dyslexia. This can be useful in reading or listening, wherein the text is converted to speech. This auditory learning mode can help students grasp and retain the acquired information. Similarly, those tools can be used by students with ADHD to organise their thoughts in a much more coherent manner and assist them in improving their writing and concentration skills.

Interactive Learning Environments AI-driven platforms provide Interactive and gamified learning for each child, whether dyslexic or ADHD. Difficulty levels can be adjusted on the fly so the learners remain challenged but calm.

AI helps sustain and motivate attention by providing an exciting and interactive way of learning—an essential ingredient in keeping interest and motivation sustained among students with ADHD symptoms.

Real-World Applications and Success Stories Many schools and institutions successfully inculcate AI tools in support of their dyslexic and ADHD students. For example, applications like Read and Write and Ghotit have functions whereby the text could be read out for the student or even be used to predict the following words to make it easier for the student to read or write.

The focused training apps for brain exercises that are applied in cognitive training to improve attention, memory, and other mind-based skills include CogniFit and Elevate, which did an excellent job for the students in managing their ADHD. Most parents and educators note a remarkable improvement in comprehension, general performance, and involvement with the study.

Such technologies support learning and make it possible to empower students with dyslexia and ADHD to become independent learners.

Challenges and Considerations

At the same time, there are a few challenges with AI solutions: majorly, the issue of accessibility will crop up, as every student might not have access to such technologies. Further, adopting AI tools in the curricula takes training and support from educators. The human touch in education is equally important; therefore, this should be preserved. Technology becomes a tool that should complement but not be a substitute for the great experiences teachers and students go through in their interactions.

For instance, AI can create far more inclusive spaces for learning, especially for kids dealing with learning differences like dyslexia or ADHD. With such technologies, present-day educators and parents can provide much-needed tailor-made support to such learners.

With the development of AI in education, applications developed in the domain are to be duly adopted in classrooms worldwide to enable all students to realise their fullest potential.

AI-Powered Learning Tools for Dyslexia

AI-intuitive educational tools may greatly help improve the reading and writing skills of dyslexic learners. Thus, relevant AI-powered apps and software can be designed for exercise and drill on such points of weakness, even cutting down the difficulty level as the learner progresses in real-time. For example, with the help of text-to-speech (TTS) technology, texts can be read aloud to students who have dyslexia, enabling them to process information in an auditory manner, not visual.

This would be helpful not only at the level of comprehension but also during reading because it bypasses the decoding stage, which is burdensome for dyslexic students. In addition, artificial intelligence will assist in writing in a predictive text form, and grammar-correcting tools will lower the powerful barrier dyslexic students face when translating ideas into the written language.

The tools learn from the user's writing style and can suggest words and phrases that speed up and improve writing.

AI-Driven Focus and Organization Aids for ADHD Attention deficit hyperactivity disorder (ADHD) is common among students, and it often prevents them from staying concentrated on tasks and even their thoughts. AI can easily handle all these issues.

AI-based applications help build an individual learning path with appropriate recreation, interactive elements, and incentives to avoid a loss of focus in a student. These tools break the material into smaller, more manageable learning bits to ease task focus. The materials are made accessible and less overwhelming to learn.

Additionally, AI can offer organisational aids tailored to students with ADHD.

For example, AI is applied in intelligent planners and to-do list applications, which use the technology to prioritise tasks depending on the user's deadlines and working pace. The technology also sends reminders and motivational messages so the student can remain on course. This can be particularly helpful for older students managing more complex schedules and workloads.

Adaptive Learning Environments AI technologies are at the forefront of developing personalised adaptive learning environments for students with learning differences. Machine learning algorithms in educational software can adapt to the pace and sometimes even adopt the learner's peculiar idiosyncratic style in real-time.

This is realised through an analysis of the student's interaction with the material and may, therefore, involve providing, for example, more visual aids for such students or interactive spelling activities to be accomplished.

These adaptive environments ensure that learning is always at the right level of challenge and encourage, but do not overwhelm, the student. They can point out success in real-time, providing positive reinforcement that is important to building a learner's confidence and motivation with dyslexia and ADHD.

Enhancing Engagement Through Gamification In learning, gamification refers to those elements used in educational applications that trigger increased motivation and engagement. Gamified AI applications can be of immense help to learners with ADHD, who generally prove to be abnormally poor regarding attention and interest in the typical non-gamified learning environment.

Such applications will make the learning process even more interactive and enjoyable since they contain rewards and give positive motivation for the work done, the task fulfilled, and the knowledge mastered.

Gamification for dyslexic students may be viewed as reading and writing practice with fun, which decreases the tension or opposition level to learning. AI will significantly support the rich field of dyslexia and ADHD with excellent features like learning personalisation and engagement, organisational tools, etc.

AI will, therefore, help educators and parents to a large extent in affording the environments to accommodate such learners and offer the necessary support for the students in question to excel.

Developments within AI technology hold vast potential in revolutionising learning for people with dyslexia and ADHD, promising a future where educational needs falling under the purview of special pedagogical considerations are indeed met with understanding and innovation.

17 | ARTIFICIAL INTELLIGENCE in Education

An educational setting tailored for students with dyslexia and ADHD, where AI technology plays a central role in facilitating a customised and engaging learning experience.

The Evolution of AI in Modern Education

Artificial intelligence currently applies in health, communication, transport, agriculture, and education, among other fields. Here, I shall investigate its potential to change how students learn and discuss how AI shapes the classroom for teachers, students, and parents.

Artificial Intelligence is a sub-discipline of computer science that involves simulating intelligent behaviours in computers and their capacity to mime, which, in ideal cases, improves human behaviour. At its heart, AI simulates how humans think, learn from experiences, make deductions, and solve problems.

The development and innovation of technology, especially artificial intelligence, have contributed significantly to making it much easier for instructors to discharge their duties more effectively and efficiently.

Technological innovations have become part of most academic sectors. In this regard, they help foster effectiveness and efficiency in education so that students enjoy their experiences by assisting with administrative chores and introducing new teaching methods.

AI is essential for freeing teachers from repetitive activities like grading students' exercises and planning lessons, allowing them to be more productive in tending to students. On the other hand, AI tools can enable the analysis of big data and provide much information on students' strengths, areas of improvement, and learning habits. In that line, teachers can customise their teaching methodology for better results.

In many instances, we have seen students benefit from AI that adapts to their pace, preferences, and learning style, opening up new learning paths that help learners exploit their talents and potential to the maximum. AI's other advantage for the student in class includes developing their analytic and problem-solving skills through interactive simulations and real-life applications.

Additionally, parental involvement is an essential factor in the success of integrating AI into education. In such a case, it will follow that parents understand AI and, in return, successfully participate in their children's learning, therefore fostering a collaborative environment. This should also involve using AI tools to track children's learning process and recommend increasing student learning.

On the other hand, parents should be well-informed about AI's boundaries and broad ethical considerations. Make the parents aware and let them decide what's best for their children's learning.

Basic Concepts of AI: Machine Learning, Natural Language Processing

Artificial Intelligence (AI) is a collection of efforts or attempts to enable a machine or a computer to do tasks that reflect human intelligence. The base is to allow machine programming to think and act in ways that reflect the human being. It is a multidisciplinary domain with interfaces that prove AI has its roots from everywhere, be it computer science, cognitive science, or linguistics.

AI development from embryonic form to the current version reflects significant strides in computation power and algorithmic invention. This development has enabled machines to execute highly complex tasks with increased independence from human control, increasing operating efficiency.

Machine Learning (ML) Definition and Foundational Concepts

Machine Learning is the core of Artificial Intelligence, a subfield completely dedicated to formulating algorithms that enable computers to learn and adapt to new data without being programmed for any task in particular. The main idea of ML is to construct models that can make reasonable predictions or decisions based on the analysis of patterns in data.

Varieties of ML

Supervised Learning: Training the algorithm with pre-labelled data to make predictions from historical input/output pairs.

Unsupervised Learning: The algorithms in this method try to find structures in unlabelled data clusters with similar points without any pre-guidance.

Reinforcement Learning: The algorithm here becomes more qualified about interacting with an environment toward the objective.

Basic Core Algorithms and Their Application: These are some of the many algorithms employed by ML, from decision trees to neural networks and support vector machines. Their applications span all domains, from simple chores like spam detection to complex problems such as voice recognition, autonomous driving, and predictive healthcare diagnosis.

Natural Language Processing (NLP) Overview and Significance

Natural Language Processing combines computer linguistics and machine learning, conformed with the development of machines able to understand, interpret, and produce the human language. NLP makes perfect interaction between man and machine possible by designing interfaces that imitate communication dynamics from human to human.

Approaches and Techniques

Employing syntactic and semantic analysis techniques and sentiment evaluation, NLP processes and understands language using tokenisation, part-of-speech tagging, and entity recognition.

Real-world Applications

The application realm of NLP is vast, encompassing chatbots, language translation, and voice-activated systems, significantly enriching the digital user experience.

Additional Fundamental AI Concepts

Robotics: Marries AI with mechanical engineering to create robots that precisely execute tasks.

Computer Vision: Equips machines with the ability to interpret visual data from their surroundings.

Expert Systems: A system simulating decision-making by human expertise in specialised fields. Challenges and Ethical Issues Along with the growth of AI technologies, fundamental issues regarding data privacy, security, and even bias are arising, which point to the need to ensure a highly ethical deployment of AI. This includes promoting transparency and retaining human control over technology.

Future Trajectories: AI is on an evolutionary path, with constant research efforts leading to improving algorithms for better effectiveness, understandability, and ethical soundness. AI presents profound implications for society in a dual fashion: offering new opportunities for improving ways of life and posing challenges that must be diligently monitored.

In conclusion, with all its related elements—machine learning and natural language processing—AI is one of the most recent technological advancements. As we enter the AI era, we must find the right balance between innovation and ethical responsibility, between exploiting AI's potential to serve society and dealing conscientiously with the complexities that this brings.

The Benefits of AI in Education

Integrating Artificial Intelligence (AI) into the educational sector has ushered in a new era of learning and teaching methodologies, marked by enhanced personalisation, efficiency, and accessibility. These technological advancements benefit students, educators, and educational institutions, transforming traditional educational paradigms into more dynamic, interactive, and compelling learning experiences. Here, we explore the myriad benefits that AI brings to the field of education.

Personalised Learning Experiences
One of AI's most significant advantages in education is its ability to create personalised learning experiences for students. Through data analysis and learning algorithms, AI can adapt curriculum content to fit individual students' learning pace, style, and preferences. This personalised approach helps address learners' diverse needs, ensuring that each student can engage with the material most effectively, enhancing understanding and retention of knowledge.

Enhanced Accessibility
AI technologies make education more accessible to a broader audience, including students with disabilities and those living in remote areas. For instance, AI-powered tools can translate educational content into various languages, provide real-time subtitles for deaf learners, and adapt learning materials for students with specific learning disabilities. This inclusivity ensures that more students have the opportunity to learn and succeed, regardless of their physical location or learning capabilities.

Improved Efficiency and Productivity
By automating administrative tasks such as grading, attendance tracking, and scheduling, AI allows educators to focus more on teaching and less on paperwork. This saves time and increases their productivity, enabling them to provide more individualised

attention to their students. Additionally, AI can quickly analyse vast amounts of educational data, providing insights that educators can use to improve their teaching strategies and enhance learning outcomes.

Support for Teachers
AI tools can serve as valuable resources for teachers, offering support in lesson planning, student assessment, and classroom management. Intelligent tutoring systems can assist in providing targeted practice where students need the most help, allowing teachers to address learning gaps more effectively.

Furthermore, AI can offer recommendations for educational resources based on the curriculum and individual student needs, making it easier for teachers to find and utilise the best materials for their classrooms.

Data-Driven Insights
AI enables the collection and analysis of data on student engagement, performance, and learning patterns. These insights can be invaluable for teachers and educational institutions in understanding the effectiveness of teaching methods and materials. By identifying trends and areas for improvement, educators can make informed decisions that enhance the quality of education and promote better academic outcomes.

Encouraging Lifelong Learning
AI-powered platforms facilitate continuous and self-directed learning, accommodating the schedules and learning preferences of individuals beyond traditional classroom settings. This promotes a culture of lifelong learning, where individuals can access educational resources and learning opportunities at any stage of their lives, adapting to the evolving demands of the job market and personal development goals.

Scalability
AI solutions can be scaled to accommodate the needs of a growing number of learners without a proportional increase in

educational resources or teaching staff. This scalability is particularly beneficial in regions with limited access to quality education, enabling more students to receive personalised and high-quality educational experiences.

The benefits of AI in education are profound and far-reaching. AI technology offers personalised learning experiences, enhances accessibility, improves efficiency, and supports teachers and educational institutions.

As AI technology continues to evolve, its integration into educational systems worldwide promises to further revolutionise the learning and teaching landscape, making education more effective, inclusive, and accessible.

Application of AI in Education	
Administration	<ul><li>Perform administration tasks faster, which consumes instructors' time for grading and feedback</li><li>Helps build personalised learning plans</li><li>Assists instructors in decision support and data-driven work.</li><li>Give feedback and work with students in a timely and direct.</li></ul>
Instruction	<ul><li>Predict student performance in projects and exercises and the odds of failure.</li><li>Analyse course material to propose customised content.</li><li>Tailor teaching method for each student based on their data.</li><li>Help instructors create personalised learning plans for each student.</li></ul>
Learning	<ul><li>Point out the learning shortcomings of students and address them in early education.</li><li>Customise the university course selection for students.</li><li>Predict the career path for each student by gathering studying data.</li><li>Detect learning state and apply intelligent adaptive intervention to students.</li></ul>

CHAPTER 2

Trends in AI-Enhanced Education

Advanced artificial intelligence (AI) essentially transforms the educational landscape. It's advancing progress in sophistication is a part of the world's educational systems that AI technologies are adopting very fast, determining future teaching and learning systems. Some key trends in this evolution can illustrate how AI has an increased influence on enhancing educational experiences. This brief paper will discuss some predominant trends in AI-boosted education, demonstrating how technology and pedagogy are combined.

Personalised and Adaptive Learning

One of the trends that could have a powerful impact is the move towards personalised learning experiences. AI-driven platforms and applications can analyse student learning habits, performance data, and preferences to mould educational content accordingly. This individualised approach facilitates the learning environment for them to work at their own pace and increases massive issues related to engagement and understanding.

Automated Administrative Tasks

AI is increasingly being applied to streamline administrative operations in educational institutions. Most operations take a lot of time, especially grading, attendance, and scheduling, among other resources. Today, these are automated through the deployment of AI technologies, raising the efficiency of operations.

Intelligent Tutoring Systems

The third is developing and deploying intelligent tutoring systems (ITS), quickly making serious inroads. The AI systems provide personalised tutoring services to learners, including feedback and recommendations tailored to the needs of a single learner. Thirdly, they are meant to help and improve traditional classroom teaching by simulating the guidance of a human tutor so that equally accessible and scalable high-quality education is provided.

Enhanced Content Delivery through AR and VR

Augmented reality (AR) and virtual reality (VR), powered by AI, reinvent content delivery into more interactive and engaging experiences. Most exciting is your very own virtual lab. Institutions are catching on with VR and AR's blossoming technology.

Indeed, some new technologies are currently being used to develop virtual labs, historical simulations, and other experiential learning environments that interest students in ways that traditional methods cannot. This applies to science, history, and languages, where understanding is context- and experience-driven.

Data-Driven Decision Making

The use of AI enables data-based decision-making for educational institutions. Artificial intelligence processes an enormous student performance and engagement database, giving

insights helpful to educators and administrative personnel for well-based curriculum development, teaching strategies, and mainly
resource allocation decisions. This will improve the effectiveness and responsiveness of educational practice.

Emphasis on Emotional and Social Learning

The cognitive, emotional, and social learning aspects are slowly searching for answers among the vast emerging AI technologies. Such AI-driven systems give educators feedback on learner emotional status and student engagement levels. Such information can help an educator adjust to enhance the students' well-being when teaching methods are changed.

This only underlines the whole fact of education being truly holistic, with equal emphasis on emotional and social skills alongside academics.

Lifelong and Ubiquitous Learning

AI provides platforms for limitless learning, where people are not restricted by place or time. In this line, AI can design platforms that offer users opportunities for continuing education in a lifelong, professional, and personal enhancement perspective at any time they need across the age brackets. This trend reflects changing workforce needs and the importance of ongoing education in a fast-changing global economy.

The developments in AI-edited education continue to underline the ever-increasing role of technology in education. From personalised learning experiences to data-driven decision-making, AI transforms how educational content is offered, managed, and assessed.

As these trends develop, they promise to democratise education further, making it more accessible.

Adaptive Learning Technologies

With technology now integrated into almost every aspect of our lives, education has not been left behind, and drastic changes have been observed, significantly regarding the advent of adaptive learning technologies. At its core, adaptive learning is an approach that uses computer algorithms to govern the interaction with the learner. It even presents resources and learning activities adapted to the student's needs.

The Essence of Adaptive Learning

Adaptive learning technologies are at the crossroads of education and innovation. The dynamic approach contrasts with the traditional model of one size fits all. These technologies are designed to adapt in real-time, depending on the learner's performance and engagement, to ensure that every student can learn in his style, at his own pace, and with content dynamically adapted to his developing needs.

The essence of adaptive learning is a learning approach that provides personalised learning for an individual through the help of technology—a manner of adapting educational or learning content and approaches to the abilities and pace of the learner.

This is the traditional one-size-fits-all model of education, to some extent, in opposition, which gives dynamism and interactivity to such a degree that, in real-time, it modifies the performance and the degree of involvement of the student. So, let's proceed to the central constituent part - the substance - which forms the essence of adaptive learning:

Personalisation

The adaptive learning systems apply algorithms to track the learners' learning interactions, responses to questions, and performance, from which they can source information about their strengths and weaknesses, learning pace, and learning styles. It is such an approach that bases its data on letting the system present the right content most adequate for the learner's level of understanding during that time and subsequently change the level of difficulty in the material later presented for review. This will mainly serve the element of personalisation, ensuring learners are not bored by accessible content or discouraged by very challenging content.

Real-Time Feedback and Adjustments

The most important feature of adaptive learning is the provision of quick feedback to learners. This allows the learners to know their mistakes on the spot, making it easy and fast to learn and correct. Based on that feedback, the system iteratively adapts an instructional strategy to ensure that the learning path is optimised for the student's ever-changing needs.

Engagement and Motivation

Adaptive learning systems keep high levels of engagement and motivation in the learner, as the learning process remains always challenging but accomplished. The personalised approach ensures that students stay focused on the topic because it refers to their level of knowledge and skill at any given time.

Most adaptive learning systems also motivate students through gamified learning, which uses points and badges to tap into intrinsic and extrinsic motivation.

Efficient Learning In such a scenario, adaptive learning maximises the efficiency of the learning process. It cuts time and effort by focusing on areas where the learner must improve while avoiding areas they have already mastered.

That efficiency quickens the learning process and ensures thorough learning of the subjects, considering that they will take longer to deal with their shortcomings. There are adaptive learning systems that gather massive data about the learners' interactions.

These can be analysed to develop valuable information regarding learning patterns, the effect of content, and general progress. This can give feedback on teaching effectiveness and point out areas needing additional materials or adjustment methods.

Moreover, this data can help predict learner outcomes, allowing for early intervention when necessary.

Scalability

While the traditional form of personalised education is resourceful in terms of time and instructor attention, the adaptive learning system can scale this personalisation to reach many learners at a go. Through technology, such systems can provide every student with a tailored learning experience around the globe.

Continuous Improvement

Adaptive learning becomes not static but evolving: the system becomes brighter and finer from learners' interaction. Ongoing feedback and improvement allow the development of increasingly effective educational tools that adapt to changing learners' needs.

Adaptive learning is, in fact, at the centre of a more individualised, flexible, and valuable form of teaching afforded by the forefront of technological education. It further prescribes a step toward understanding and servicing learners' needs to create an inclusive, participative, and pragmatic learning experience.

The technological advance and the promised possibility of adaptive learning in transforming educational paradigms raise the probability that learners who centre on needs and potential will arise.

Why Adaptive Learning Matters

Adaptive learning technologies promise to make modern educational practices much more effective. They also make students hope for more personalised learning. Students will finally not be passive recipients of information but active participants in a learning journey tailor-made for them. Adaptive learning thus supports multi-style and multi-pace learning for students, making them feel their learning. The approach is practical for students to learn independently and profoundly.

Besides, adaptive learning technologies are valuable tools for teachers and educators to provide insights into every learner's deep-trenched learning processes. These data-informed approaches help the educator identify areas where the students may struggle or excel; hence, the instruction and intervention are more laser-focused.

Standing on the verge of a new epoch in education, adaptive learning technologies are a promising forerunner of the world where learning is more than knowledge transfer but probably a customised journey of discovery and growth for each student. Heading in that direction, it subscribes to an educational model where each learner is considered worthy and prepared with all it takes to survive in a world that will offer change at every turn.

Historical Background of Adaptive Learning Technologies

The journey of adaptive learning technologies from concept to classroom intertwines with the evolution of educational theories and technological advancements. This historical voyage reveals a steadfast ambition to personalise education, ensuring that learning aligns with each student's unique needs, pace, and preferences.

The Early Beginnings

Originating in the middle of the 20th century, adaptive learning **took** its roots when programmed instruction and teaching machines **existed**. These early attempts, inspired by the work from Skinner's **behaviourist psychology, took** shape **by individualising** the learning process through mechanical means. In the meantime, the work of great pioneers such as Skinner allowed students to work through a set of questions at a pace of their own, receiving instant feedback regarding the accuracy of their answers.

The Transition to Digital

Of course, when computers appeared, and later the Internet, the adaptive learning technologies also changed—the new millennium brought with it the advent of sophisticated software in education with the use of algorithms that can very well analyse student data and generate from the analysis a personalised learning experience for the student.

Further into this era, there was further development in computer-based training (CBT) systems, intelligent tutoring systems (ITS), and learning management systems (LMS), which were the first to manifest into what today can be termed adaptive learning platforms.

The Rise of AI and Machine Learning

What has distinguished the latest chapter in the history of adaptive learning technologies is the incorporation of artificial intelligence (AI) and machine learning. These technologies have enhanced adaptive systems' capacities to analyse large pools of student learning behaviour data in ways that allow adjustments to the curriculum to be made more subtly and, therefore, more effectively than ever before. AI-powered platforms can predict student performance, knowledge gaps, precision, and personal learning pathways at an unprecedented level.

Historical context for developing adaptive learning technologies: an ongoing endeavour to harness emerging technologies as potential tools that may enhance more personalised, effective, and engaging educational experiences. From Skinner's teaching machines to the current era of AI adaptive learning, this transition is a realisation of improvements in technology and how it is used to cater to different learner needs.

Explore Specific Examples of Adaptive Learning Technologies in Use Today

Adaptive learning technologies have woven their way into educational experiences across various platforms and institutions. Below, we explore specific examples that highlight the diversity and impact of these technologies in enhancing learning outcomes.

1. Knewton

Knewton was one of the pioneers in adaptive learning, offering a platform that customises educational content for students based on their needs. While Knewton has evolved, its legacy continues to influence the development of adaptive learning solutions that analyse student interactions and performance to tailor the learning experience.

2. DreamBox Learning

DreamBox Learning provides an adaptive math program for kindergarten through eighth-grade students. Its intelligent adaptive learning technology assesses each student's responses and automatically adjusts the difficulty level of math problems and lessons accordingly. DreamBox's in-depth reporting tools also allow educators and parents to track student progress in real-time.

3. Smart Sparrow

Bright Sparrow is an adaptive eLearning platform that allows educators to create rich, interactive courses that adapt to learners' responses. It supports various disciplines and offers educators the tools to design personalised learning pathways, incorporating simulations, adaptive feedback, and branching scenarios.

4. ALEKS

ALEKS (Assessment and LEarning in Knowledge Spaces) is a web-based, artificially intelligent assessment and learning system that uses adaptive questioning to determine what a student knows in a course and then instructs the student on the topics they are most ready to learn. ALEKS is widely used in mathematics, chemistry, and statistics.

5. Duolingo

While primarily known as a language learning app, Duolingo employs adaptive learning technologies to customise lessons for each user. Its algorithm assesses a learner's performance and tailors future exercises to improve language skills effectively, making it a popular tool for personalised language education.

These examples represent just a fraction of the adaptive learning technologies available today, offering unique approaches to Personalising education. By harnessing the power of data analysis and artificial intelligence, these platforms demonstrate the potential of adaptive learning to create more engaging, effective, and tailored educational experiences for learners worldwide.

Benefits and Challenges of Adaptive Learning Technologies

Adaptive learning technologies have heralded a new era in education, offering personalised learning experiences that can significantly enhance student engagement and outcomes. However, like any transformative technology, they come with their own set of challenges. Below, we explore the benefits and the hurdles associated with these technologies.

Benefits

1. **Personalized Learning Experiences**

- Adaptive technologies tailor learning content and pace to the individual learner, accommodating different learning styles and needs. This personalisation helps to ensure that all students can engage with the material in a way that best suits them, potentially leading to improved understanding and retention of knowledge.

2. **Enhanced Student Engagement**
    - Adaptive learning technologies can help keep students motivated and engaged by providing content at the right difficulty level and interest for each student. Interactive elements and feedback can further enhance this engagement, making learning more enjoyable and effective.

3. **Data-Driven Insights**
    - These technologies offer educators and institutions valuable insights into student performance and learning patterns. This data can inform teaching strategies, curriculum development, and early intervention for students who may be struggling, making education more responsive and effective.

1. **Integration with Existing Systems**
    - Integrating adaptive learning technologies into existing educational frameworks and systems can be complex and costly. Schools and institutions may need to invest in new infrastructure and training for educators to use these technologies effectively.

2. **Data Privacy and Security**
    - The collection and analysis of student data raise significant privacy and security concerns.

Ethically protecting and using personal information requires robust security measures and transparent policies.

3. **Ensuring Depth of Learning**
    - While adaptive technologies excel at personalising learning experiences, focusing on individual learning paths could lead to a fragmented understanding of the subject matter. Educators must ensure that personalised learning complements broader educational goals and outcomes.

4. **Accessibility and Equity**
    - Socioeconomic factors, including the availability of internet access and digital devices, can limit access to adaptive learning technologies. Ensuring that these technologies do not widen the educational divide but instead serve to make learning more accessible to all students is an ongoing challenge.

Adaptive learning technologies hold promise for much, if not all, of the quest toward realising fuller, more individualised, engaging, and practical education. However, additional challenges must be addressed to fully capitalise on that potential and meaningfully achieve a required level—above and beyond the previously alluded to. The strategies for successful implementation will likely change along with these technologies, but the future of education will be highly learner-oriented and include individualised opportunities.

Conclusion and Future Outlook on Adaptive Learning Technologies

Indeed, as we have moved through the realms of adaptive learning technologies—from historical roots to payoffs and challenges presented—one thing is clear: These tools are not some passing fancy in education. This, in turn, presents a significant shift toward a more personalised, data-driven, and, where needed, flexible learning environment. These are the challenges and many others that these new adaptive learning technologies will need to face and right themselves where at all possible to allow for a better future with the use of them.

The Path Forward

The trajectory of adaptive learning technologies is poised for significant growth, driven by advancements in artificial intelligence, machine learning, and data analytics. As these technologies become more sophisticated, we can expect adaptive learning platforms to offer even more nuanced and compelling personalisation, catering to individual student's specific learning styles, preferences, and needs.

Embracing Challenges as Opportunities

The challenges highlighted earlier, such as integration issues, data privacy concerns, ensuring depth of learning, and accessibility, will necessitate innovative solutions.

The future of adaptive learning will depend on the ability of educators, technologists, and policymakers to collaborate on creating secure, effective, and equitable learning environments that Leverage adaptive technologies' strengths while mitigating their limitations.

A Vision for Inclusive, Lifelong Learning

Looking ahead, adaptive learning technologies can democratise education, making high-quality, personalised learning experiences accessible to students worldwide, regardless of their geographical location or socioeconomic status.

Moreover, as lifelong learning becomes increasingly important in a rapidly changing world, these technologies can provide flexible, on-demand learning opportunities for individuals at all stages of life and careers.

Final Thoughts

The journey of adaptive learning technologies is a testament to the ongoing quest for a more personalised and practical educational experience. As we move forward, the focus must remain on harnessing these technologies to serve the diverse needs of learners, empowering them to achieve their full potential. The future of education is not just about technology; it's about creating learning environments that are more responsive, engaging, and inclusive than ever before.

Reflecting on Improvements for Adaptive Learning Technologies

As adaptive learning technologies continue to evolve, there are several areas where improvements can significantly enhance their effectiveness and impact. Addressing these areas helps overcome some of the current challenges and unlocks the full potential of adaptive learning to revolutionise education. Here are some critical areas for improvement:

Enhancing Algorithmic Transparency and Ethical Considerations.

Algorithmic Transparency: Increasing the transparency of the algorithms used in adaptive learning systems can help educators and learners Understand how decisions are made. This transparency can build trust and allow more informed use of these technologies.

Ethical Considerations:

Developing ethical guidelines for using student data and designing adaptive learning experiences is crucial. These guidelines must ensure fairness, avoid biases in algorithmic decisions, and protect learner privacy.

Improving Integration and Interoperability

Seamless Integration: Streamlining the integration of adaptive learning technologies with existing educational systems and infrastructures can reduce barriers to adoption. This involves developing standards and protocols that allow for easy integration without significant overhauls of current systems.

Interoperability:

Enhancing the interoperability of adaptive learning systems with various platforms and tools used in education can facilitate a more cohesive learning ecosystem. This allows sharing data and insights across platforms, enriching the learning experience.

Broadening Access and Equity

Increasing Accessibility: Adaptive learning technologies must be accessible to diverse learners, including those with disabilities. This means designing inclusive interfaces and content that comply with accessibility standards.

Addressing the Digital Divide:

Efforts to mitigate the digital divide by providing necessary hardware, software, and internet access can ensure that adaptive learning technologies benefit all students, regardless of their socio-economic background.

Fostering Deeper Learning and Critical Thinking

Promoting Critical Thinking:

While adaptive technologies excel at personalising learning paths, there is room for improvement in promoting critical thinking and problem-solving skills. Incorporating scenarios and tasks that challenge students to apply knowledge in new and complex situations can enhance more profound learning.

Balancing Adaptive Learning with Human Interaction:

It is, therefore, of great importance that one strikes the balance between technology-driven learning and human contact in this manner. Adaptive learning should include collaboration, discussion, and feedback opportunities from the educator and his peers to help the student have an all-inclusive experience from traditional education methods.

The improvement of adaptive learning technologies requires an approach that looks into the technical, ethical, and pedagogical problems, which can better live up to the promise to transform education. Such technologies can ensure an approach focusing on transparency, integration, accessibility, and promotion of deeper learning. Thus, the future of adaptive learning will be in building systems that are not only smart and responsive but fair, accommodating, and able to prepare learners for the complexities that modern life subjects them to.

AI-Driven Analytics in Student Performance

The era of educational analytics, particularly student performance, is on the verge of being revolutionised by the advent of artificial intelligence (AI). The other term related to e-portfolio 2 is "AI-driven analytics." AI-driven analytics is the implementation of artificial intelligence technologies to collect, study, and interpret students' learning behaviours and achievements. This breakthrough uniquely informs the learning process since it uncompromisingly informs educators about how to adapt instructional strategies and, if necessary, interventions should be done.

The Significance of AI in Modern Education

The significance of AI-driven analytics in education must be considered. Teachers might rely on periodic assessments, observations, and student feedback to gauge learning outcomes in a traditional educational setting. While valuable, these methods offer limited granularity and often must catch up to students' real-time needs. AI-driven analytics changes this dynamic, providing a continuous, automated stream of data that captures the nuances of each student's learning journey.

By leveraging machine learning algorithms and big data technologies, AI-driven analytics can identify patterns and trends that might elude human observers. This includes pinpointing specific areas where students struggle, predicting future performance based on past behaviour, and recommending personalised learning paths that cater to each learner's unique strengths and weaknesses. The ultimate goal is to foster a learning environment where every student can achieve their full potential, supported by insights derived from their data.

Transforming Education through Personalization and Efficiency

One of the most compelling aspects of AI-driven analytics is its ability to personalise education at scale. Personalisation is critical to ensuring that no student is left behind in a classroom of diverse learners, each with their learning styles, paces, and preferences. AI-driven analytics facilitates this by automatically adjusting learning content, difficulty levels, and instructional strategies based on real-time data. This enhances student engagement and motivation and optimises the learning process for efficiency and effectiveness.

Moreover, AI-driven analytics empowers educators with a powerful toolset to streamline their efforts. Instead of spending extensive time on administrative tasks or manual data analysis, teachers can focus on what they do best: inspiring, guiding, and mentoring their students. With AI handling the heavy lifting of analytical tasks, educators are free to devote more attention to the creative and interpersonal aspects of teaching that are vital for student growth and development.

As we stand on the threshold of a new era in education, AI-driven analytics offers a glimpse into a future where data-driven insights and personalised learning are not just ideals but everyday realities. By harnessing the power of artificial intelligence, we can unlock new possibilities for student achievement, transforming how education is delivered and experienced for generations to come.

Exploring the Mechanics of AI-Driven Analytics

The mechanics of AI-driven analytics in education are grounded in interconnected processes that collect, analyse, and interpret vast amounts of data to enhance student learning and performance. This intricate system leverages various artificial intelligence components, including machine learning algorithms, natural language processing, and predictive analytics, to provide actionable insights into student behaviour and achievements. Here's a closer look at how these components transform education.

Data Collection Methods

1. **Learning Management Systems (LMS):** These platforms serve as the primary data source, capturing detailed information on student interactions, including assignment submissions, quiz scores, forum participation, and time spent on different tasks.

2. **Educational Apps and Tools:** Many educational technologies integrate with AI analytics to offer a more nuanced view of student engagement, such as problem-solving approaches in math apps or reading patterns in literacy software.

3. **Sensors and Biometrics:** In some advanced implementations, sensors and biometric devices collect data on student attentiveness, emotional responses, and even physical engagement during learning activities.

Analysis and Interpretation

1. **Machine Learning Algorithms:** These algorithms analyse the collected data to identify patterns, trends, and anomalies. For example, they can detect if a student consistently struggles with a particular problem or concept, indicating areas where additional support is needed.

2. **Natural Language Processing (NLP):** NLP analyses text-based interactions, such as essays and discussion posts, assessing content quality, sentiment, and engagement levels. This helps in understanding students' comprehension and emotional states.

3. **Predictive Analytics:** By applying statistical models to historical and real-time data, predictive analytics can forecast future student performance, allowing educators to intervene proactively with at-risk students.

Personalisation and Adaptation

1. **Adaptive Learning Pathways:** Based on the analysis, AI systems can automatically adjust the learning content, difficulty level, and instructional methods to match the student's current needs and learning pace.

2. **Feedback and Recommendations:** AI-driven analytics provide personalised feedback and recommendations to students, guiding them through their learning journey with tailored advice on study strategies, resources, and review topics.

3. **Dynamic Curriculum Adjustment:** In more advanced systems, the curriculum can adapt in real-time, introducing new topics or reinforcing previous ones based on collective class performance data.

The Impact of AI-Driven Analytics

The mechanics of AI-driven analytics represent a significant leap forward in educational technology. By systematically collecting and analysing data, these systems offer personalisation and adaptability previously unattainable in traditional academic settings. The result is a more responsive, efficient, and effective learning environment where students are not only consumers of information but active participants in a personalised educational journey tailored to their needs.

This approach enhances student engagement and motivation and provides educators with powerful tools to identify and address learning gaps, optimise instructional strategies, and ultimately improve educational outcomes for all students.

Mechanics of AI-Driven Analytics in Student Performance

The mechanics of AI-driven analytics in student performance encompass a sophisticated blend of data collection, analysis, and personalisation techniques. These components work harmoniously to transform raw educational data into actionable insights, paving the way for personalised and adaptive learning experiences. Let's investigate these mechanisms to understand how AI revolutionises the academic landscape.

Data Collection Methods

The foundation of AI-driven analytics is built on comprehensive data collection. This involves gathering information on various aspects of student performance, including but not limited to:

- **Engagement metrics:** Time spent on tasks, participation in discussions, and interaction with learning materials.

- **Assessment results:** Scores from quizzes, tests, and other evaluation forms.

- **Behavioural data:** Patterns of study, frequency of logins, and use of educational resources.

- **Feedback inputs:** Responses to surveys, instructor feedback, and peer evaluations.

Advanced sensors and learning management systems (LMS) seamlessly integrate into digital learning environments, facilitating the continuous collection of this data without disrupting the learning process.

Analysis and Interpretation

Once collected, the data undergoes analysis and interpretation using AI algorithms and machine learning models. These tools can process vast amounts of information and identify patterns and correlations that may take time to be apparent. Key processes include:

- **Pattern recognition:** Identifying common pathways through which students achieve success or encounter difficulties.

- **Predictive analytics:** Forecasting future performance based on historical data, enabling early intervention for at-risk students.

- **Adaptive learning algorithms:** Modifying learning content and pathways in real-time based on student progress and preferences.

This analytical process is crucial for understanding the complexities of learning behaviours and tailoring educational experiences to individual needs.

Personalisation and Adaptation

The ultimate aim of AI-driven analytics is to facilitate personalised and adaptive learning. This is achieved by applying the insights gained from data analysis to create dynamic learning environments that respond to the individual learner. Key aspects include:

- **Customized learning paths:** These paths adjust the sequence and difficulty of learning activities to match the learner's pace and proficiency level.

- **Targeted content delivery:** Presenting content in formats that align with the learner's preferred learning style, whether textual, visual, auditory, or interactive.

- **Feedback and interventions:** Providing timely and constructive feedback and recommended actions to overcome learning obstacles.

Through these mechanisms, AI-driven analytics enhances the learning experience. It empowers students to take charge of their educational journey, fostering a deeper engagement with the material and promoting long-term knowledge retention.

The mechanics of AI-driven analytics represent a confluence of technology and pedagogy, offering a nuanced approach to understanding and improving student performance. By leveraging data in all its forms, AI opens new vistas for personalised education, making it possible to meet the unique needs of every learner. As these technologies Evolve, so will the opportunities to enrich and transform the educational landscape.

Explore Real-World Applications and Case Studies of AI-driven analytics in Education.

AI-driven analytics in education is not just a theoretical concept but a practical reality transforming learning experiences across the globe. By examining specific applications and case studies, we can appreciate the tangible impact of these technologies on student performance and educational outcomes. Let's explore some noteworthy examples.

1. Personalized Learning at Scale: Carnegie Learning

Carnegie Learning's adaptive learning platform, powered by AI, offers a compelling case study in personalised education. Their math programs use sophisticated algorithms to adapt to each student's responses in real time, tailoring instruction to their specific needs. This approach has been shown to significantly improve math scores in diverse school districts, demonstrating the power of AI to enhance learning outcomes on a large scale.

2. Early Identification of At-Risk Students: Georgia State University

Georgia State University employs an AI-driven alert system to identify students at risk of failing or dropping out. By analysing data on grades, attendance, and engagement, the system flags students who may need additional support, enabling timely intervention. This proactive approach has dramatically reduced dropout rates and closed achievement gaps, showcasing how AI analytics can be used to support student success beyond the classroom.

3. Enhancing Language Learning: Duolingo

Duolingo, a popular language learning app, uses AI to customise learning experiences for millions of users worldwide. Its AI algorithms analyse user data to optimise lesson difficulty and content, ensuring learners remain engaged and progress at their own pace. Duolingo's success illustrates the potential of AI-driven analytics to make language learning more accessible and effective for a global audience.

4. Improving Writing Skills: Turnitin's Revision Assistant

Turnitin's Revision Assistant uses AI to provide students with immediate, actionable feedback on their writing. The tool analyses student essays against a vast database of writing samples, offering suggestions for improvement on clarity, coherence, and grammar. This instant feedback loop helps students refine their writing skills more efficiently, highlighting the role of AI in supporting the development of critical academic skills.

5. Adaptive Testing: GRE and GMAT

The Graduate Record Examination (GRE) and the Graduate Management Admission Test (GMAT) are notable for their use of computer-adaptive testing, where the difficulty of the test adjusts based on the test-taker's performance. This application of AI-driven analytics ensures that the tests accurately measure the abilities of individuals across a wide range of skill levels, providing a more personalised and fair assessment method.

These case studies demonstrate the diverse applications of AI-driven analytics in education, from personalised learning and early intervention to language learning and adaptive testing. By leveraging the power of AI, educators and institutions can provide more engaging, effective, and personalised educational experiences.

As technology advances, we can anticipate even more innovative applications of AI in education, further enhancing student learning outcomes worldwide.

Automated Grading and Feedback Systems

Automated grading systems have been implemented in various forms across educational institutions and online platforms. These systems showcase the potential of technology to support and enhance the assessment process. Here are some specific examples of automated grading systems that have significantly impacted.

1. **Turnitin**

Turnitin is best known for its plagiarism detection capabilities but offers automated grading and feedback features. Turnitin's "Feedback Studio" provides instructors with tools to grade assignments and exams quickly using automated and manual comments. It uses advanced algorithms to identify grammar, spelling, and punctuation errors and offers suggestions for improvement.

2. **Grammarly**

While primarily a tool for improving writing through grammar, punctuation, and style suggestions, Grammarly's advanced AI algorithms offer potential applications for automated grading in educational contexts. Analysing text for clarity, engagement, and delivery can provide instant feedback that can be leveraged in grading student writing assignments.

3. **EdX and Coursera**

Online learning platforms like EdX and Coursera utilise automated grading systems to manage the massive volume of coursework from students worldwide. These platforms sometimes employ AI to grade quizzes, programming assignments, and written responses. The automated feedback and grading allow them to offer courses at scale, including those with subjective assessment components.

4. Knewton

Knewton's adaptive learning platform includes features for automated assessment and feedback. By analysing student performance data, Knewton provides personalised recommendations and adjustments to the learning path, including automated grading assignments and quizzes. This system exemplifies how adaptive learning and automated grading can be integrated to enhance personalised learning experiences.

5. Project Essay Grade (PEG)

PEG is an automated essay-scoring system developed by Measurement, Inc. It evaluates the quality of written work by analysing more than 500 features, including fluency, diction, grammar, and construction. PEG demonstrates how AI can be applied to assess complex assignments like essays, providing scores that correlate strongly with human grading.

Future Directions

The evolution of automated grading systems is closely tied to advancements in AI and machine learning technologies. These systems will likely offer even more accurate and nuanced grading capabilities as they become more sophisticated. Future developments could include:

- **Improved Natural Language Understanding:** Enhanced AI models that better grasp the subtleties of human language and writing styles.

- **Greater Integration with Learning Management Systems:** Seamless integration with LMS platforms to provide a more cohesive educational experience.

- **Ethical and Bias-Mitigation Algorithms:** Advanced algorithms designed to identify and mitigate potential biases in grading, ensuring fairness and objectivity.

Through their diverse applications and capabilities, automated grading systems illustrate AI's potential to revolutionise educational assessment. By providing efficient, consistent, and personalised feedback, these systems support educators and students in learning. As technology advances, the scope and effectiveness of automated grading will continue to expand, opening new possibilities for its application in education.

Integration of Automated Grading with Adaptive Learning Platforms

Integrating automated grading systems with adaptive learning platforms represents a powerful synergy in educational technology, offering a dynamic, personalised learning experience that can significantly enhance student outcomes. This integration leverages both technologies' strengths to create an environment where learning is continually optimised based on real-time performance data. Let's explore how this integration works and its benefits for education.

How Integration Works

1. **Real-Time Data Collection:** Adaptive learning platforms continuously collect data on student interactions, responses, and time spent on various tasks. When integrated with automated grading systems, these platforms can incorporate assessment results into their data pool, offering a more comprehensive view of student performance.

2. **Dynamic Feedback and Assessment:** Automated grading provides immediate feedback on assignments and assessments to the adaptive learning platform. This immediate response allows the platform to adjust the learning path in real-time, tailoring the difficulty level and presenting new material optimally for each student's learning progress.

3. **Personalized Learning Paths:** The platform can identify patterns, strengths, weaknesses, and learning preferences based on the combined data from adaptive learning interactions and automated grading feedback. It then uses this information to create a highly personalised learning path for each student, ensuring they are constantly engaged with challenging yet achievable material.

Benefits of Integration

1. **Enhanced Personalization:** The integration allows for a level of personalisation that is difficult to achieve through traditional teaching methods. Students receive a customised learning experience that adapts not just to their learning style but also to their mastery of the content.

2. **Improved Student Engagement:** With real-time feedback and challenges tailored to their current level of understanding, students are more likely to stay engaged and motivated. This increased engagement can lead to higher retention rates and better learning outcomes.

3. **Efficient Resource Allocation:** This integration means that educators can more effectively focus their time and resources. They can quickly identify struggling students who need additional support, while students who excel can be provided with more advanced materials to keep them challenged.

4. **Data-Driven Insights:** The wealth of data generated through this integrated approach offers profound insights into the learning process, allowing educators and institutions to make informed decisions about curriculum development, teaching strategies, and resource allocation.

Future Prospects

Integrating automated grading with adaptive learning platforms is still evolving, with future advancements likely to offer even more significant benefits. Potential developments include:

- **Advanced AI Models:** More sophisticated AI models could provide deeper insights into student learning styles and preferences, further enhancing personalisation.

- **Broader Application Range:** Expanding the range of subjects and skills that can be assessed and taught through these integrated platforms, including soft skills and complex problem-solving.

- **Improved Feedback Mechanisms:** Developing more nuanced feedback mechanisms that offer constructive criticism and suggestions akin to a human instructor.

Integrating automated grading systems with adaptive learning platforms marks a significant advancement in the use of technology in education. By combining the efficiency and scalability of automated grading with the personalised approach of adaptive learning, this integration can significantly improve educational outcomes. As technology evolves, the possibilities for creating more adaptive, responsive, and effective learning environments are boundless.

Ethical Considerations of Automated Grading

Adopting automated grading systems in education raises important ethical considerations that must be addressed to ensure fairness, privacy, and students' overall well-being. While these systems offer numerous benefits, including efficiency and the ability to provide instant feedback, their implications on educational integrity, student privacy, and equity are significant. Let's explore these ethical considerations in detail.

Bias and Fairness

1. **Algorithmic Bias:** Like any AI-driven technology, automated grading systems can inherit biases in their training data or algorithms. This can lead to unfair grading practices where specific student demographics are systematically disadvantaged.

2. **Transparency and Explainability:** These systems often need more transparency in their grading decisions, making it difficult for students and educators to understand or challenge the results. They ensured that automated systems were explainable, and their justifiable choices were crucial for maintaining trust.

Privacy and Data Security

1. **Student Data Privacy:** Automated grading systems collect and analyse vast student data. Ensuring the privacy and security of this data is paramount to protecting students from potential misuse or breaches.

2. **Consent and Ownership:** Questions about who owns the data and how consent is obtained are central to ethical considerations. Students and educators must clearly understand how data is used and the ability to opt-out if desired.

Impact on Learning and Pedagogy

1. **Over-reliance on Automation:** There's a risk that an over-reliance on automated grading could devalue the importance of human feedback in the learning process. The nuanced input from educators, crucial for developing critical thinking and creative skills, may be overshadowed by the efficiency of automated systems.

2. **Standardization vs Creativity:** Automated systems often rely on standardised grading criteria, potentially stifling

creativity and penalising unconventional thinking. Balancing the need for objective assessment with encouraging creative responses is a critical ethical challenge.

Equity and Access

1. **Digital Divide:** The effectiveness of automated grading systems is predicated on technology access. This raises concerns about equity for students with unreliable internet access or digital devices, exacerbating existing educational inequalities.

2. **Adaptability to Diverse Educational Contexts:** Automated systems must be adaptable to various educational settings and needs, including accommodations for students with disabilities. Ensuring these systems are inclusive and equitable is a significant ethical consideration.

Future Directions

Addressing these ethical considerations requires ongoing dialogue among educators, technologists, policymakers, and students. Future directions may include:

- **Developing Ethical Frameworks:** Establishing clear ethical guidelines for developing and using automated grading systems to ensure they are fair and transparent and respect student privacy.

- **Enhancing Algorithmic Accountability:** Implementing measures to audit and rectify algorithm biases, ensuring that automated grading systems are equitable and fair to all students.

- **Promoting Hybrid Approaches:** Encouraging automated grading as a complement to, rather than a replacement for, human assessment to preserve the invaluable elements of educator feedback and mentorship.

The ethical considerations surrounding automated grading systems are complex and multifaceted. By carefully navigating these issues, stakeholders can harness the benefits of these technologies while minimising their potential drawbacks, ensuring that automated grading serves as a tool for enhancing, rather than diminishing, educational equity and quality.

CHAPTER 3

AI in Curriculum Development

Integrating Artificial Intelligence (AI) into curriculum development is revolutionising the educational landscape, offering new methodologies for designing, implementing, and updating educational content better to meet the needs of students and educators alike. This integration represents a significant shift towards more dynamic, personalised, and effective educational experiences. Let's delve into how AI shapes curriculum development, its benefits, challenges, and the prospects of this exciting intersection.

AI can analyse vast amounts of data regarding student learning patterns, preferences, and outcomes, providing invaluable insights that can guide curriculum development. This data-driven approach enables educators to tailor learning experiences to their students' unique needs, ensuring that educational content is relevant, engaging, and aligned with desired learning outcomes.

Key Areas of Impact

1. **Personalized Learning Paths:** AI algorithms can design curriculum paths that adapt to each student's learning pace and style, suggesting content that addresses specific strengths and weaknesses.

2. **Content Optimization:** AI can help identify which parts of the curriculum are most effective and which need

improvement, allowing for real-time content updates and enhancements.

3. **Predictive Analytics:** AI can predict future learning trends and outcomes by analysing student performance data, helping educators proactively adjust the curriculum to meet emerging needs.
4. **Interactive and Adaptive Learning Materials:** AI facilitates the creation of dynamic learning materials that adjust based on student interactions, providing an immersive and adaptive learning experience.

Benefits of AI in Curriculum Development

1. **Enhanced Engagement and Retention:** Personalized and adaptive curricula designed by AI increase student engagement and knowledge retention by presenting material that aligns with each student's learning preferences.
2. **Efficiency in Curriculum Design:** AI streamlines the curriculum development process, automating the analysis of educational content effectiveness and student feedback, thereby reducing the time and resources required.
3. **Data-Driven Decision Making:** AI in curriculum development allows educators and institutions to make informed decisions based on comprehensive data analysis, improving educational outcomes.

Challenges and Considerations

1. **Ethical and Privacy Concerns:** The collection and analysis of student data raise significant privacy concerns, necessitating stringent data protection measures and ethical guidelines.

2. **Depersonalization Risk:** Over-reliance on AI could deplete education, underscoring the need to maintain human elements in teaching and curriculum development.
3. **Accessibility and Equity:** Ensuring that AI-driven curriculum development tools are accessible to all students, regardless of socioeconomic status, is critical in avoiding widening educational disparities.

Future Prospects

The future of AI in curriculum development is promising, with potential advancements including:

- **More Sophisticated Personalization Algorithms:** Future AI systems could offer more nuanced personalisation, accommodating a broader range of learning styles and needs.
- **Integration with Emerging Technologies:** Combining AI with virtual reality (VR) and augmented reality (AR) could create immersive and interactive curricula.
- **Continuous Learning Systems:** AI could enable the development of curricula that evolve in real-time, adapting to individual learners and changing societal and industry needs.

AI's role in curriculum development is transformative, offering pathways to more personalised, efficient, and practical education. While challenges remain, particularly concerning ethics and equity, the potential benefits of AI in creating dynamic and responsive educational experiences are immense. As AI technologies evolve, so will how we design and implement curricula, heralding a new era of data-driven education.

Figure 3 Here's an image that envisions AI's role in curriculum development within a modern, collaborative workspace.

Examples of AI-Driven Curriculum Development

Integrating artificial intelligence (AI) in curriculum development transforms educational paradigms and offers more personalised, dynamic, and efficient learning pathways. AI-driven curriculum development uses algorithms and machine learning models to design, implement, and adapt educational content and teaching methodologies based on student data, performance, and feedback. Here are some notable examples of how AI is being used to revolutionise curriculum development across various educational settings.

1. **Content Technologies (Content Technologies, Inc., Cram101)**

Content Technologies, Inc. (CTI) uses AI to transform textbooks into engaging learning experiences. Their product, Cram101, utilises AI to summarise textbook content into digestible study guides, practice tests, and flashcards. This approach allows educators to quickly develop curriculum materials tailored to their courses' specific needs and learning outcomes, ensuring that students can access concise, relevant, and personalised learning aids.

2. **Carnegie Learning**

Carnegie Learning's adaptive learning platform is renowned for its math curriculum that dynamically adjusts to each student's learning pace and style. By leveraging AI and cognitive science, the platform provides real-time data and analytics to educators, enabling them to identify gaps in knowledge and adjust the curriculum accordingly. This AI-driven approach ensures that the curriculum remains responsive to the needs of the students, fostering a more effective and personalised learning environment.

3. **ALEKS (Assessment and Learning in Knowledge Spaces)**

ALEKS is an adaptive learning system that uses AI to assess student knowledge in mathematics, chemistry, and accounting. It then tailors the curriculum to meet the unique needs of each learner by identifying which topics they are ready to learn based on their current knowledge state. ALEKS is an example of how AI-driven curriculum development can create a personalised learning path that continually adapts to the progress and performance of each student.

4. **Smart Sparrow**

Bright Sparrow is an adaptive eLearning platform that allows educators to create custom interactive courses. The AI in Smart Sparrow analyses student responses to adapt the curriculum in real time, offering personalised pathways through the content. This technology enables educators to design curricula catering to diverse learning styles and speeds, making learning more engaging and effective.

5. IBM Watson Education

IBM Watson Education uses AI to provide educators with insights into learning habits and competencies at an individual and class level. By analysing data on student performance and engagement, Watson can recommend adjustments to the curriculum, ensuring that it aligns with students' needs and learning progress. This AI-driven approach to curriculum development supports a more dynamic and responsive educational experience.

AI-driven curriculum development is paving the way for educational experiences that are increasingly personalised, engaging, and effective. By leveraging AI to analyse student data and adapt the curriculum in real time, these technologies ensure that learning materials always align with students' individual needs and capabilities. As AI technology evolves, its role in curriculum development is expected to grow, offering new opportunities to enhance education and learning outcomes.

The Impact of AI-Driven Curriculum on Teacher Roles

Integrating Artificial Intelligence (AI) in curriculum development significantly reshapes teachers' roles and responsibilities. While AI offers innovative tools for personalised learning and efficient curriculum design, it also prompts a re-evaluation of the teacher's role in the classroom. Here's how AI-driven curriculum development is impacting educators and their pedagogical approaches.

Facilitators of Learning

Teachers are transitioning from traditional lecturers to facilitators of learning. AI-driven curricula can handle personalised content delivery, allowing teachers to focus more on guiding students through their learning journey, fostering critical thinking, and facilitating discussions. This shift emphasises the teacher's role in nurturing a supportive learning environment that encourages exploration and inquiry.

Interpreters of Data

AI technologies provide a wealth of data on student performance and learning patterns. Teachers are increasingly required to interpret this data to make informed decisions about pedagogical strategies. This involves understanding the insights generated by AI systems, such as identifying areas where students struggle or excel and using this information to tailor classroom activities and interventions.

Designers of Learning Experiences

This will enable teachers to create unique learning experiences that go well with AI-complemented content, for most of the curriculum development is an output of AI. Development examples in a unit of work include project-based learning activities, collaborative group work, and real-world problem-solving tasks that apply the curriculum meaningfully. Teachers might make meaningful steps toward enhancing students' engagement, deepening their understanding, and developing these critical skills, which AI cannot teach. Among these skills are empathy, leadership, and teamwork.

Lifelong Learners

As AI's application in education continues to grow, every teacher will be a learner by practice. Educators must keep learning and updating their skills and knowledge to effectively integrate these AI tools into their teachings. They learn to use new AI-guided platforms in the latest education technologies and adapt to new pedagogical models, taking advantage of AI.

Ethical Guides and Mentors

This involves educating teachers to instil an ethical mind toward technology as AI infiltrates education. It discusses digital citizenship, data privacy, and the need for all AI users to use their data ethically. Teachers will also act as mentors, taking learners through the careful digital world and teaching them how to evaluate information and instruments at their disposal critically. The evolution of AI-enabled curriculum development is not diluting the worthy role of teachers; on the contrary, it adds value to the scenario by paving the way for newer opportunities for teachers to work on and influence students in alternative dimensions.

It provides teachers the headroom to focus on the more human-centred aspects of teaching, such as emotional support, ethical guidance, and soft skills development. At the same time, AI stands in the gap for personalised content delivery and data analysis. As the learning environment increasingly changes through technology, the teacher's role as a guide, mentor, and the lifelong learner becomes more critical to student success.

Strategies for Integrating AI-Driven Curriculum in Traditional Classrooms

Integrating an AI-driven curriculum into traditional classroom settings requires thoughtful planning and execution to maximise its benefits while minimising disruptions. Here are strategies educators and institutions can employ to blend AI tools with existing educational practices seamlessly.

1. **Professional Development and Training**
    - **Educator Training:** Provide comprehensive training for educators on using AI-driven tools and interpreting data insights. This ensures they are comfortable and proficient with the technology, enabling them to integrate it effectively into their teaching.
    - **Continuous Learning:** Encourage ongoing professional development opportunities to update educators on AI advancements and pedagogical strategies.

2. **Gradual Implementation**
    - **Pilot Programs:** Start with pilot programs to test AI-driven curriculum tools in a controlled environment. This allows for adjustments based on feedback and performance before broader implementation.
    - **Incremental Integration:** Gradually integrate AI tools into the curriculum, starting with subjects or areas where AI can have the most immediate and positive impact. This helps teachers and students acclimate to the new tools.

3. **Student-Centric Approach**
    - **Personalized Learning Paths:** Use AI to create personalised learning experiences that cater to the needs and pace of individual students. This approach can help bridge learning gaps and enhance student engagement.
    - **Empowering Students:** Teach students how to interact with AI-driven tools and take charge of their learning journey. This includes training on digital literacy and responsible technology use.

4. Infrastructure and Support

- **Technology Infrastructure:** Ensure that the necessary technology infrastructure, including hardware and reliable internet access, is in place to support AI-driven curriculum tools.

- **Technical Support:** Provide robust technical support for educators and students to address issues quickly, minimising downtime and frustration.

5. Collaboration and Feedback

- **Stakeholder Collaboration:** Involve all stakeholders, including educators, students, parents, and IT staff, in the implementation process. Their insights can help tailor the integration strategy to meet the community's needs.

- **Feedback Loops:** Establish mechanisms for regular feedback from users of AI-driven tools. This feedback is invaluable for refining the technology and its integration into the classroom.

6. Ethical and Privacy Considerations

- **Data Privacy:** Implement strict data privacy policies to protect student information. Educators should understand these policies and be able to communicate them to students and parents.

- **Ethical Usage:** Educate educators and students on the ethical use of AI in education, emphasising the importance of critical thinking and the limitations of technology.

7. Blending Traditional and AI-Enhanced Methods

- **Hybrid Models:** Develop hybrid models that blend traditional teaching methods with AI-driven tools. This can include combining in-person lectures with AI-facilitated personalised learning activities.

- **Human Element:** Ensure that integrating AI tools does not replace the invaluable human interaction between teachers and students. The goal is to enhance, not replace, traditional educational experiences.

Integrating AI-driven curriculum into traditional classrooms requires a balanced approach considering technological, pedagogical, and ethical aspects.

By providing adequate training, ensuring infrastructure support, involving all stakeholders, and adopting a student-centric approach, educators can leverage AI to enrich learning experiences without losing the essence of traditional education.

Challenges and Ethical Considerations of AI in Curriculum Development

While promising, integrating Artificial Intelligence (AI) in curriculum development presents several challenges and ethical considerations that must be addressed to ensure its effective and responsible use. These concerns range from technical limitations to broader ethical issues affecting students, educators, and the educational system. Understanding and addressing these challenges is crucial for leveraging AI to enhance academic outcomes ethically and sustainably.

Technical and Practical Challenges

1. **Data Quality and Bias:** AI systems use large datasets to learn and make decisions. In curriculum development, biased or poor-quality data can lead to inaccurate or unfair content recommendations, potentially reinforcing stereotypes or marginalising certain groups of students.

2. **Interoperability and Integration:** Integrating AI tools with existing educational technologies and curriculum frameworks can be challenging. Issues with compatibility, data silos, and the seamless flow of information can hinder the effective use of AI in curriculum development.

3. **Scalability and Accessibility:** While AI can personalise learning at scale, ensuring that these technologies are accessible to all students, regardless of their socio-economic background or geographical location, remains challenging.

Ethical Considerations

1. **Privacy and Data Security:** AI in education involves collecting, analysing, and storing vast amounts of personal data from students. This raises significant concerns about privacy and the security of student information, especially in light of potential data breaches or misuse.

2. **Transparency and Accountability:** AI algorithms' decisions affecting curriculum development and student learning must be transparent. With clear explanations, assessing their fairness or holding providers accountable for biased outcomes can be more accessible.

3. **Informed Consent:** Students and parents must be informed about how student data is used in AI-driven curriculum development. This includes understanding what data is collected, how it is used, and the ability to opt out if desired.

4. **Depersonalization of Education:** While AI can offer personalised learning experiences, there is a risk of depersonalising education by over-relying on technology

at the expense of human interaction and the social aspects of learning.

5. **Equity and Inclusivity:** Ensuring that AI-driven curriculum development benefits all students equally is a primary ethical consideration. This includes addressing the digital divide and ensuring that AI tools do not exacerbate educational inequalities.

Future Directions

Addressing these challenges and ethical considerations requires a collaborative effort among educators, technologists, policymakers, and the broader educational community. Potential strategies include:

- Developing ethical guidelines and standards for the use of AI in education.
- Investing in research to understand the impacts of AI on learning outcomes and equity.
- Implementing robust data privacy protections and transparent data practices.
- Encouraging the development of AI tools that complement rather than replace human teachers.

AI in curriculum development offers exciting possibilities for personalising and enhancing education. However, realising its full potential requires navigating a complex landscape of technical challenges and ethical considerations. By addressing these issues proactively, the educational community can harness the power of AI to create more effective, equitable, and engaging learning experiences for all students.

Integration of AI-Driven Curriculum in Non-Traditional Educational Settings

Integrating Artificial Intelligence (AI) into curriculum development extends beyond traditional classroom environments, offering transformative possibilities for non-traditional educational settings. These settings include online learning platforms, homeschooling environments, vocational training programs, and adult education centres. Let's explore how AI-driven curricula can be integrated into these non-traditional settings to enhance learning experiences and outcomes.

Online Learning Platforms

1. **Personalized Learning Paths:** AI can analyse learner data to create personalised learning paths, adapting the curriculum to each individual's strengths, weaknesses, and learning pace. This personalisation is particularly beneficial in online learning, where learners have diverse backgrounds and needs.

2. **Automated Feedback and Assessment:** AI-driven systems provide immediate feedback on assignments and quizzes, allowing learners to understand their progress and areas for improvement in real time. This feature supports a more dynamic and interactive online learning experience.

Homeschooling Environments

1. **Customized Curriculum Development:** AI tools can assist parents and guardians in developing customised curricula that align with their child's interests, learning styles, and educational goals. This approach ensures that homeschooling can be as targeted and effective as traditional schooling methods.

2. **Resource Recommendations:** AI can recommend educational resources, activities, and supplementary materials based on the learner's progress and interests, helping homeschooling parents curate a rich and varied educational experience.

Vocational Training Programs

1. **Skills Gap Analysis:** AI can analyse job market trends and identify skills gaps, allowing vocational training programs to tailor curricula to meet current and future industry needs. This ensures that learners are equipped with relevant skills that enhance their employability.

2. **Simulation-Based Learning:** In vocational training, AI-driven simulations can provide hands-on learning experiences that mimic real-world scenarios. This approach allows learners to practice and hone their skills in a controlled, risk-free environment.

Adult Education Centres

1. **Flexible Learning Schedules:** AI-driven platforms can offer flexible learning schedules that accommodate the busy lives of adult learners. By allowing learners to progress at their own pace, AI ensures that education is accessible and manageable for those balancing work, family, and study.

2. **Career Transition Support:** AI can guide relevant courses and learning pathways for adults looking to change careers or upskill. By analysing labour market data, AI helps adult learners make informed decisions about their education and career development.

Challenges and Considerations

While integrating AI-driven curriculum in non-traditional settings offers numerous benefits, it also presents challenges such as ensuring equitable access to technology, addressing data privacy concerns, and maintaining the quality and relevance of educational content. Addressing these challenges requires concerted efforts from educators, policymakers, and technology providers to create inclusive, effective, and secure learning environments.

Integrating AI-driven curriculum in non-traditional educational settings represents a significant opportunity to make learning more personalised, accessible, and aligned with individual needs and goals. By leveraging AI, these settings can overcome traditional barriers to education, offering learners of all ages and backgrounds the chance to achieve their full potential. As AI technologies evolve, their role in shaping innovative and inclusive educational experiences will expand.

AI in Educational Assessment

Artificial Intelligence (AI) in educational assessment revolutionises how educators evaluate student learning, progress, and outcomes. AI technologies are being leveraged to create more efficient, accurate, and personalised assessment methods. Below, we explore various aspects of AI's role in educational assessment, including its applications, benefits, and challenges.

Applications of AI in Educational Assessment

1. **Automated Essay Scoring (AES):** AI algorithms can evaluate written responses, grading them not just on grammar and syntax but also on the coherence, logic, and creativity of the argument. Tools like Turnitin's Grade scope and ETS's e-rater are examples of AES in action.

2. **Adaptive Testing:** AI can dynamically adjust the difficulty of test questions based on the test taker's performance in real-time, ensuring a more accurate assessment of their knowledge and skills. This approach is utilised in standardised tests like the GRE and GMAT.

3. **Performance Assessment:** Beyond traditional testing, AI can assess students' performance in simulations, games, and virtual environments. This is particularly useful in vocational training and STEM education, where practical skills are as essential as theoretical knowledge.

4. **Continuous Assessment:** AI systems can monitor student interactions with learning materials, providing ongoing assessments that give a more comprehensive picture of the student's progress over time. This continuous feedback loop supports a more nuanced understanding of learning trajectories.

Benefits of AI in Educational Assessment

1. **Personalization:** AI enables personalised assessment, tailoring questions and tasks to the student's learning level and style. This ensures that evaluations are accessible and challenging, enhancing the learning experience.

2. **Efficiency:** AI-driven assessments can be administered and graded automatically, saving time for educators and providing immediate feedback to students. This efficiency allows for frequent assessments, offering regular insights into student progress.

3. **Objectivity:** By standardising the assessment process, AI can help reduce biases and human error, leading to more objective and fair evaluations of student performance.

4. **Data-Driven Insights:** The data collected through AI assessments can offer deep insights into student learning

patterns, helping educators identify areas of strength and weakness. This information can inform targeted interventions and support strategies.

Challenges and Ethical Considerations

1. **Validity and Reliability:** It is critical to ensure that AI assessments accurately measure their intended evaluation. Questions about the validity and reliability of AI-driven assessments must be addressed to ensure they genuinely benefit learning.

2. **Equity and Access:** Reliance on AI in assessment could exacerbate existing inequalities if not all students have equal access to the necessary technology or if the AI algorithms are not trained on diverse data sets.

3. **Data Privacy:** The use of AI in assessment involves collecting and analysing vast amounts of personal data, raising significant privacy concerns. Safeguarding this data and ensuring it is used ethically is paramount.

4. **Dependence on Technology:** Overreliance on AI for assessment could undermine the development of critical human judgment skills in educators and students alike. Balancing AI use with human oversight is crucial.

AI is transforming educational assessment, offering tools for more personalised, efficient, and objective evaluations of student learning. However, maximising the benefits of AI in assessment while addressing its challenges requires careful implementation, ongoing evaluation, and a commitment to ethical principles. As AI technology evolves, so will its potential to enhance educational assessment practices, promising a future where assessments align more with individual learner needs and academic goal

AI's Impact on Special Education

Integrating Artificial Intelligence (AI) into special education opens up new avenues for supporting students with diverse needs. AI technologies offer personalised learning experiences, adaptive educational materials, and innovative support tools that can significantly enhance the educational outcomes for students with disabilities. Here's how AI is making a difference in special education:

Personalised Learning Experiences

1. **Adaptive Learning Platforms:** AI-driven platforms can adjust lessons' content, pace, and complexity to match the unique learning profiles of students with special needs. This personalisation ensures that learning experiences are tailored to individual abilities and challenges, making education more accessible and practical.

2. **Speech and Language Therapy:** AI applications in speech and language therapy can provide personalised exercises and real-time feedback, helping students with speech and language impairments improve their communication skills more efficiently.

Assistive Technologies

1. **Communication Aids:** AI-powered communication aids assist non-verbal students or those with speech difficulties in expressing themselves. Devices and apps that use AI to convert text or symbols into speech enable these students to communicate more effectively.

2. **Visual Assistance:** For students with visual impairments, AI-driven tools can describe visual content, read text aloud, and even guide them through physical spaces, enhancing their learning experience and independence.

Behavioural and Emotional Support

1. **Behavioural Analysis:** AI can analyse data on student behaviour to identify patterns or triggers for specific actions. This information can help educators develop personalised strategies to support students with behavioural challenges.

2. **Emotional Recognition:** AI technologies recognise and respond to emotional cues and can support students with emotional and social challenges. These tools can help educators understand and address students' emotional states, promoting a more supportive learning environment.

Challenges and Considerations

While AI offers significant potential benefits for special education, several challenges and ethical considerations must be addressed:

1. **Accessibility and Inclusivity:** It is crucial to ensure that AI technologies are designed to be accessible and usable by all students, including those with severe disabilities. This requires inclusive design practices and ongoing user testing.

2. **Data Privacy:** AI in special education involves sensitive data on students' learning abilities, behaviours, and health information. Protecting this data and ensuring its ethical use is paramount.

3. **Teacher Training and Support:** Educators need appropriate training and support to integrate AI tools into special education effectively. This includes understanding how to use these technologies and interpret the data they provide.

4. **Cost and Resource Allocation:** The cost of advanced AI technologies may be prohibitive for some schools or districts, potentially creating disparities in access to these resources. Addressing these financial challenges is essential to ensure equitable access to AI benefits.

AI has the potential to transform special education by providing personalised learning experiences, innovative assistive technologies, and valuable behavioural and emotional support. By addressing the associated challenges and ethical considerations, educators and policymakers can leverage AI to support the diverse needs of students with disabilities, promoting inclusion and enhancing educational outcomes in unique education settings.

AI's Role in Teacher Professional Development

Artificial Intelligence (AI) is revolutionising how students learn and transforming professional development for teachers. AI can significantly enhance teachers' skills and teaching methods by providing personalised learning experiences, real-time feedback, and access to educational resources. Here's how AI is impacting teacher professional development:

Personalised Learning for Teachers

1. **Customized Professional Development Plans:** AI can analyse a teacher's classroom performance, student feedback, and professional interests to create personalised professional development (PD) plans. These plans can focus on areas where the teacher wants to grow, such as classroom management, innovative teaching methods, or subject matter expertise.

2. **Adaptive Learning Platforms for Teachers:** Just as students benefit from adaptive learning, teachers can use similar platforms for their PD. These platforms can adjust content and challenges based on the teacher's learning pace and evolving needs, ensuring that PD is practical and engaging.

Real-Time Feedback and Coaching

1. **AI-Powered Coaching Tools:** AI tools can offer real-time feedback on classroom instruction by analysing video recordings or live feeds of teaching sessions. These tools can highlight strengths and areas for improvement, offering actionable insights that teachers can use to refine their techniques.

2. **Virtual Reality (VR) Simulations:** VR simulations powered by AI can provide immersive PD experiences, allowing teachers to practice classroom management,

student engagement strategies, and pedagogical approaches in a safe, controlled environment. Feedback from these simulations can help teachers develop new skills without the fear of making mistakes in a real classroom.

Access to Global Resources and Collaboration

1. **AI-Curated Educational Content:** AI can curate and recommend the latest research, teaching strategies, and educational technologies based on the teacher's interests and professional goals. This ensures teachers can access the most current and relevant information in their field.

2. **Facilitating Collaboration:** AI-driven platforms can connect teachers with peers worldwide, facilitating collaboration and the exchange of ideas. These platforms can recommend connections based on shared interests, teaching subjects, or professional goals, creating a global professional learning community.

Challenges and Ethical Considerations

While AI offers promising opportunities for enhancing teacher PD, there are several challenges and ethical considerations to address:

1. **Equity and Access:** Ensuring all teachers have equal access to AI-powered PD resources, especially in under-resourced schools or regions, is crucial.

2. **Data Privacy:** Protecting the privacy of teachers' performance data and feedback is essential to maintaining trust and ensuring that AI tools are used ethically.

3. **Quality and Relevance:** The quality and relevance of AI-recommended resources and feedback must be continually assessed to ensure they meet teachers' diverse needs.

4. **Balancing Technology with Human Interaction:** While AI can provide personalised learning and feedback, the value of human mentors, coaches, and peer collaboration should not be underestimated. Balancing AI tools with human elements is critical to effective PD.

AI has the potential to significantly enhance teachers' professional development by offering personalised learning experiences, real-time feedback, and access to global resources. By addressing the associated challenges and ethical considerations, educational institutions can leverage AI to support teachers in their continuous professional growth, ultimately leading to improved teaching practices and student outcomes.

CHAPTER 4

Challenges of Integrating AI in Education

Integrating Artificial Intelligence (AI) into education brings many benefits, including personalised learning experiences, enhanced efficiency in administrative tasks, and new insights into pedagogical effectiveness. However, this integration also raises significant ethical considerations and privacy concerns that must be carefully navigated to protect students, educators, and the integrity of the educational process. This exploration delves into the critical ethical and privacy issues surrounding the use of AI in education and proposes strategies for addressing these challenges.

Ethical Considerations

Bias and Fairness

AI systems, including those used in education, can inadvertently perpetuate and amplify biases in their training data. This can lead to unfair treatment of students based on race, gender, socioeconomic status, or disabilities. Ethical integration of AI in education requires rigorous testing and monitoring for bias, ensuring that AI tools promote fairness and inclusivity.

Transparency and Accountability

AI systems' decision-making processes can be opaque, making understanding how they arrive at certain conclusions or recommendations difficult. This lack of transparency in educational settings can affect stakeholder trust and accountability, particularly when decisions impact student outcomes. Ensuring that AI systems are explainable and their choices can be audited is crucial.

Impact on Student Autonomy and Learning Experience

AI-driven personalisation in education tailors learning experiences to individual students' needs. However, there's a fine line between personalisation and over-reliance on technology, which can impede students' ability to learn independently and develop critical thinking skills. Striking a balance that enhances learning while preserving student autonomy is a vital ethical challenge.

Privacy Concerns

Data Privacy and Security

AI in education often involves collecting, storing, and analysing vast amounts of personal data, including sensitive information about students' learning habits, performance, and even biometric data. Protecting this data against unauthorised access and ensuring its security is paramount. Educational institutions must adhere to strict data privacy laws and regulations, such as GDPR in Europe and FERPA in the United States, and employ robust cybersecurity measures.

Consent and Data Ownership

Obtaining informed consent from students and parents for data collection and analysis is critical to ethical AI integration. Stakeholders should be informed about what data is collected, how it is used, and who owns it. Furthermore, students and parents should be allowed to opt out of data collection without negative consequences.

Surveillance and Monitoring

The potential for AI tools to be used for surveillance and continuous monitoring of students raises significant privacy concerns. This includes tracking students' online activities, physical whereabouts, and emotional states. Such practices can infringe on students' rights to privacy and freedom, creating a culture of surveillance rather than support.

Addressing Ethical and Privacy Concerns

1. **Develop and Implement Ethical Guidelines:** Educational institutions should develop comprehensive ethical guidelines for AI use that address bias, transparency, accountability, and student autonomy.

2. **Prioritize Data Privacy and Security:** Implementing strong data protection measures and ensuring compliance with relevant privacy laws are essential. This includes encrypting data, limiting access, and conducting regular security audits.

3. **Promote Transparency and Informed Consent:** AI tools and their use in education should be transparent, and informed consent should be obtained from students or guardians. Stakeholders should have access to information about the AI systems and their implications.

4. **Foster a Culture of Ethical AI Use:** Educators, administrators, and policymakers should be trained to use AI ethically in education. This includes understanding the limitations of AI tools and prioritising human judgment when necessary.

Integrating AI into education offers tremendous opportunities to enhance learning and administrative efficiency. However, navigating the ethical considerations and privacy concerns associated with its use is crucial to ensuring that these technologies Benefit all students equitably and maintain the trust and integrity of the educational environment.

The Impact of AI on Educational Policy

Integrating Artificial Intelligence (AI) into the educational sector prompts significant shifts in educational policy as governments, institutions, and stakeholders recognise the need to adapt regulatory frameworks to harness AI's benefits while mitigating potential risks. This multifaceted impact influences how educational content is delivered, assessed, and managed. Below, we explore the various dimensions of AI's impact on educational policy.

Policy Adaptations for AI Integration

1. **Privacy and Data Protection:** Because AI relies on data, educational policies increasingly focus on protecting student privacy. This involves creating or updating data protection regulations to cover the collection, storage, and use of student data by AI systems, ensuring compliance with transparency, consent, and security principles.

2. **Equitable Access:** AI technologies have the potential to personalise learning and make education more accessible. Policies are being developed to promote equitable access to AI-enhanced education, address the digital divide, and ensure that AI tools do not exacerbate existing inequalities.

3. **Ethical Standards and Bias Mitigation:** As the deployment of AI in education raises ethical concerns, including the potential for bias in AI algorithms, policies are being formulated to establish ethical standards for AI use in educational contexts. These policies ensure fairness, accountability, and inclusivity in AI-driven educational practices.

4. **Teacher Training and Professional Development:** Recognizing the importance of teachers in effectively integrating AI into education, policy initiatives focus on teacher training and Professional development. Policies are designed to equip educators with the necessary skills to leverage AI tools in teaching and learning processes effectively.

5. **Curriculum and Assessment Reform:** AI's capabilities to provide personalised learning experiences and assess student performance in real-time are leading to curriculum design and assessment methods reforms. Educational policies are being revised to incorporate AI-driven teaching, learning, and evaluation approaches, emphasising skills relevant to the digital age.

6. **Research and Innovation Support:** Policies are being implemented to support research and innovation in AI for education. This includes funding for AI educational research, developing AI tools tailored for educational purposes, and partnerships between academic institutions and technology companies.

7. **International Collaboration:** Given the global nature of AI technology and its potential impact on education worldwide, there is a growing emphasis on international collaboration in policy development. This involves sharing best practices, developing common standards, and ensuring that the benefits of AI in education are accessible across different regions and contexts.

Challenges in Policy Development

1. **Keeping Pace with Technological Advancements:** One of the main challenges in developing educational AI-related policies is the rapid pace of technological change, which can render policies outdated shortly after implementation.

2. **Balancing Innovation with Regulation:** Finding the right balance between encouraging innovation in AI and imposing Regulations to protect students and ensure ethical use is a delicate task for policymakers.

3. **Addressing Diverse Stakeholder Interests:** In developing educational policies related to AI, the interests of various stakeholders, including students, educators, technology providers, and policymakers, must be balanced.

The impact of AI on educational policy is profound, driving significant changes in how education is delivered, managed, and assessed. As AI evolves, educational policies must adapt to ensure that integrating AI technologies into the academic sector is beneficial, equitable, and ethical. Policymakers play a crucial role in navigating these changes, requiring a forward-looking approach that anticipates future developments in AI and their potential implications for education.

The Digital Divide and Equity Access in AI in Education

Integrating Artificial Intelligence (AI) in education can revolutionise learning by providing personalised, flexible, and innovative educational experiences. However, this technological advancement raises significant concerns regarding the digital divide and equitable access to AI-enhanced education.

The digital divide refers to the gap between individuals with access to modern information and communication technology (ICT) and those without, often due to socioeconomic, geographical, or demographic factors. In the context of AI in education, this divide can exacerbate existing inequalities, making it crucial to address equity access comprehensively.

The Impact of the Digital Divide

1. **Access to Technology:** The foremost issue is the unequal access to the necessary technology, including hardware (computers, tablets, smartphones) and reliable internet connectivity. Students needing these essential resources can benefit from AI-driven educational tools, widening the educational opportunities and outcomes gap.

2. **Quality of Education:** AI can offer high-quality, personalised learning experiences that adapt to each learner's needs and pace. However, students in under-resourced communities often attend schools that need help to afford such advanced technologies, leading to disparities in the quality of education received.

3. **Skill Gaps:** The use of AI in education requires a certain level of digital literacy among students and teachers. Students need the skills to interact effectively with AI technologies to engage with or benefit from these tools.

4. **Teacher Preparedness:** Equitable access to AI in education also depends on teachers' ability to integrate

these technologies into their teaching. Schools in low-income areas may need more resources for teacher training and professional development in AI, further contributing to the digital divide.

Strategies to Bridge the Divide

1. **Infrastructure Investment:** Governments and educational institutions must invest in infrastructure that provides all students access to the Internet and digital devices. Public-private partnerships can facilitate this access, especially in remote or underserved areas.

2. **Inclusive Design and Development:** AI educational tools should be designed with inclusivity, ensuring they are accessible to students with disabilities and support multiple languages and cultural contexts. This approach can help make AI-driven education more universally accessible.

3. **Digital Literacy Programs:** Implementing digital literacy and skills training programs for students and teachers is essential. These programs can equip users with the necessary competencies to effectively utilise AI technologies in education.

4. **Policy and Regulation:** Policymakers must develop and enforce regulations that ensure equitable access to AI educational tools. This includes policies that support funding for technology in under-resourced schools and guidelines for inclusive and ethical AI development.

5. **Community Engagement:** Engaging communities in implementing AI in education can help identify specific barriers to access and develop targeted strategies to overcome them. Community-based programs can also provide additional support and resources for students and families.

While AI in education promises to transform learning experiences, addressing the digital divide and ensuring equitable access is imperative to prevent exacerbating educational inequalities.

By implementing targeted strategies and policies that focus on inclusivity, infrastructure, and digital literacy, it is possible to leverage AI to benefit all students, regardless of their background or circumstances.

Bridging the digital divide in AI education is a technical challenge and a moral imperative to ensure that technological advancements lead to equitable education improvements for everyone.

Teacher and Student Adaptability to AI Tools

Integrating Artificial Intelligence (AI) tools in education necessitates adaptability among teachers and students. This shift towards AI-enhanced learning environments brings many opportunities for personalised education, efficient classroom management, and innovative teaching and learning methods. However, it also presents challenges that require teachers and students to adapt to new roles, learn new skills, and embrace a mindset geared towards continuous learning and flexibility.

Teacher Adaptability to AI Tools

1. **Embracing New Pedagogical Roles:** As AI tools take on more administrative and instructional tasks, teachers can shift from content deliverers to facilitators of learning, mentors, and designers of complex problem-solving tasks that AI cannot handle. Adapting to this role requires a willingness to rethink traditional teaching methods and explore new ways to engage students.

2. **Developing Technological Proficiency:** Teachers must become proficient in using AI tools to integrate them into the classroom effectively. This involves learning how to operate these tools and understanding how they can enhance learning outcomes. Continuous professional development and training are essential for teachers to stay updated on the latest AI technologies and their educational applications.

3. **Interpreting Data for Personalized Learning:** AI tools can provide valuable data on student performance and learning preferences. Teachers need to adapt by developing data analysis and interpretation skills to tailor instruction to meet their students' individual needs, thereby enhancing the personalisation of learning.

4. **Fostering Ethical and Critical Engagement with AI:** Teachers play a crucial role in guiding students on the ethical use of AI tools and encouraging a critical understanding of these technologies, including their limitations and potential biases. This requires teachers to be well-informed about the ethical considerations associated with AI in education.

Student Adaptability to AI Tools

1. **Learning How to Learn with AI:** Students must adapt to new ways of learning as AI tools offer personalised pathways and adaptive learning experiences. This includes developing self-regulated learning skills, such as goal setting, time management, and self-assessment, to engage effectively with AI-enhanced education.

2. **Digital Literacy and Responsibility:** The use of AI tools necessitates a high level of digital literacy among students, including understanding how to use these tools responsibly and safely. Students must also be aware of data privacy issues and learn to protect their personal information.

3. **Collaborative Skills in an AI Environment:** While AI can support personalised learning, it offers collaborative projects and peer learning opportunities. Students need to adapt by developing skills to work effectively in teams, both in-person and in virtual environments facilitated by AI tools.

4. **Critical Thinking and Creativity:** As AI takes over more routine learning tasks, students can focus on developing higher-order thinking skills, such as critical thinking, creativity, and Problem-solving. Adapting to this shift requires students to engage deeply with content and apply their knowledge in innovative ways.

Strategies to Support Adaptability

- **Providing Training and Support:** Both teachers and students require ongoing training and support to develop the necessary skills to use AI tools effectively. Educational institutions should Offer professional development opportunities for teachers and incorporate digital literacy into the curriculum for students.

- **Creating a Culture of Continuous Learning:** Encouraging a culture that values continuous learning, experimentation, and adaptability can help both teachers and students embrace the changes brought about by AI in education.

- **Encouraging Collaboration:** Facilitating collaboration among teachers and between students can help share best practices, overcome challenges, and foster a supportive learning community adaptable to AI integration.

Teachers and students' adaptability to AI tools in education is crucial for maximising the benefits of these technologies. By embracing new roles, developing new skills, and fostering a culture of continuous learning and ethical engagement with technology, teachers and students can navigate the challenges and opportunities AI presents in education.

Data Security and Management

Integrating Artificial Intelligence (AI) in education brings a transformative potential to enhance learning experiences, personalise education, and streamline administrative processes. However, this integration also raises significant concerns regarding data security and management. As educational institutions increasingly rely on AI tools that process vast amounts of personal and sensitive data, ensuring this data's security and proper management becomes paramount. Here's how AI can play a crucial role in enhancing data security and management in the educational sector.

Enhancing Data Security with AI

1. **Automated Threat Detection:** AI systems can monitor real-time network traffic to identify and alert administrators about potential security threats or anomalies. These systems learn from historical data to recognise patterns, efficiently detecting new and sophisticated cyber threats that traditional software might miss.

2. **Predictive Analytics for Proactive Security:** By analysing patterns and trends in data access and usage, AI can predict potential security breaches before they occur. This allows institutions to proactively address vulnerabilities, such as weak access points or outdated software, reducing the risk of data breaches.

3. **Encryption and Access Control:** AI can automate the encryption of sensitive data and enforce access controls, ensuring that only authorised users can access certain information. AI algorithms can also manage complex encryption keys more efficiently than manual processes, enhancing data protection.

4. **User Behaviour Analytics:** AI tools can analyse user behaviour to identify unusual activities that may indicate a security threat, such as accessing data at odd hours or downloading large volumes of data. This helps quickly identify and mitigate insider threats.

Improving Data Management with AI

1. **Data Classification and Organization:** AI can automatically classify, tag, and organise educational data, making it easier to manage, access, and protect. This includes sorting data into categories such as personal information, academic records, and administrative documents, each with appropriate security and access controls.

2. **Data Quality and Integrity:** AI algorithms can continuously monitor data for accuracy, consistency, and completeness, identifying and correcting errors or inconsistencies. This ensures the reliability of educational data, which is crucial for making informed decisions and personalising learning experiences.

3. **Compliance Monitoring:** AI tools can help educational institutions comply with data protection regulations such as the General Data Protection Regulation (GDPR) and the Family Educational Rights and Privacy Act (FERPA). AI can monitor and document data processing activities, generate compliance reports, and alert administrators to potential compliance issues.

4. **Efficient Data Retrieval:** AI-powered search and retrieval systems can quickly locate information within vast educational databases, saving time and resources. This capability supports academic research, administrative decision-making, and personalised education by enabling quick access to relevant data.

Challenges and Considerations

While AI offers significant benefits for data security and management in education, it also presents challenges:

- **Ethical Use of AI:** Ensuring the ethical use of AI in handling educational data, particularly regarding student privacy and consent.

- **Dependence on AI:** Overreliance on AI systems could lead to vulnerabilities if those systems are compromised. Human oversight remains essential.

- **AI Security:** AI systems themselves can be targets of cyber-attacks. Securing these systems is critical to protect the data they manage and analyse.

AI presents a powerful tool for enhancing data security and management in education, offering solutions to protect sensitive information, improve data integrity, and ensure compliance with regulations. However, realising these benefits requires careful implementation, ongoing oversight, and a commitment to addressing AI technologies' ethical and security challenges. As AI continues to evolve, so will its role in safeguarding and managing the digital backbone of educational institutions.

CHAPTER 5

Prospects of AI in Education and Personalised Paths

The advent of Artificial Intelligence (AI) in education has introduced a paradigm shift towards personalised learning, offering tailored educational experiences that meet each learner's unique needs, preferences, and pace. Personalised learning pathways, facilitated by AI, represent a significant departure from the traditional one-size-fits-all approach, promising to enhance learning outcomes, engagement, and accessibility. This book explores the concept of personalised learning pathways in AI in education, examining their benefits, implementation strategies, and potential challenges.

Concept and Significance

Personalised learning pathways refer to educational trajectories that adapt to individual students' learning styles, paces, and interests. By leveraging AI, educational platforms can analyse vast data regarding students' interactions, performance, and feedback, creating customised learning experiences. This approach acknowledges and values the diversity in learners' abilities and backgrounds, aiming to optimise their educational journey.

Benefits of Personalized Learning Pathways

1. **Enhanced Engagement and Motivation:** Personalized pathways keep learners engaged by presenting content that aligns with their interests and challenges them at just the right difficulty level. This relevance and challenge are crucial to sustaining motivation and interest in learning.

2. **Improved Learning Outcomes:** Personalized pathways can improve comprehension and retention by accommodating individual learning styles and paces. Learners who receive instruction tailored to their needs are likelier to master the subject matter and achieve their educational goals.

3. **Efficient Use of Time:** AI-driven personalisation ensures that learners spend their study time effectively, focusing on areas where they need improvement and skipping over content they already understand. This efficiency can accelerate learning progress and reduce frustration.

4. **Support for Diverse Learning Needs:** Personalized pathways are particularly beneficial for learners with special needs or those who fall outside the traditional educational system's median. AI can help identify and cater to these diverse needs, offering support that is both inclusive and effective.

Implementation Strategies

1. **Data-Driven Insights:** The foundation of personalised learning pathways is data. AI algorithms analyse data on students' performance, learning behaviours, and preferences to customise their learning pathways.

2. **Adaptive Learning Technologies:** Implementing adaptive learning platforms that adjust content, difficulty, and learning modalities based on real-time student data is

crucial. These technologies can guide learners through their personalised pathway, adapting as they progress.

3. **Continuous Feedback and Assessment:** Personalized pathways rely on ongoing assessment and feedback to adjust the learning journey. AI can automate these assessments, providing immediate feedback to learners and insights to educators.

4. **Teacher and Technology Collaboration:** While AI plays a central role in personalising learning, teachers remain essential for providing support, mentorship, and intervention. Educators must work alongside AI tools, using their insights to enhance teaching strategies.

Challenges and Considerations

1. **Data Privacy and Security:** The data collection necessary for personalised learning raises concerns about privacy and security. Safeguarding student information is paramount, requiring robust data protection measures.

2. **Algorithmic Bias:** AI systems can inadvertently perpetuate biases in their training data, leading to unfair or ineffective personalisation. Continuous monitoring and adjustment of algorithms are necessary to mitigate these biases.

3. **Resource Allocation:** Developing and implementing AI-driven personalised learning pathways can be resource-intensive. Educational institutions may need help securing the necessary funding, technology, and training.

4. **Digital Divide:** Ensuring equitable access to personalised learning opportunities requires addressing the digital divide. All students must have access to the necessary technology and connectivity to benefit from AI-driven education.

Personalised learning pathways in AI in education represent a transformative approach to learning, offering the promise of more engaged, efficient, and practical education tailored to the needs of each learner. While implementing such pathways presents challenges, the potential benefits for learner outcomes and educational equity are substantial. As technology continues to evolve, so will the opportunities to refine and expand personalised learning, making it an increasingly integral part of the educational landscape.

Enhancing Student Engagement Through AI

Deploying artificial intelligence (AI) in educational settings significantly transforms learning by providing tools and strategies to enhance student engagement. Engagement, a crucial determinant of successful learning outcomes, has often been challenging across diverse learning environments and student populations. AI offers personalised, interactive, and adaptive learning experiences that can captivate students' interest and sustain their engagement over time. This detailed exploration delves into the mechanisms through which AI enhances student engagement, the benefits of such engagement, and practical examples of AI applications in fostering an engaging learning environment.

Mechanisms of AI in Enhancing Engagement

1. **Personalized Learning Experiences:** AI algorithms analyse individual learning patterns, preferences, and performance to tailor educational content, making learning more relevant and engaging for each student. This personalisation addresses learners' unique needs, helping to maintain their interest and motivation.

2. **Interactive Content:** AI-powered platforms often incorporate interactive elements such as gamification, simulations, and virtual or augmented reality experiences. These elements transform learning from passive to active,

increasing engagement through immersion and interactivity.

3. **Adaptive Learning Pathways:** AI adjusts the complexity and pacing of learning material based on real-time feedback and assessments. By presenting neither easy nor complex challenges, AI keeps students in optimal engagement, known as the zone of proximal development.

4. **Immediate Feedback and Support:** AI systems provide instant feedback on assignments and quizzes, allowing students to understand their mistakes and learn from them immediately. This immediate reinforcement helps maintain students' interest and encourages a growth mindset.

Benefits of Enhanced Engagement through AI

1. **Improved Academic Performance:** Higher engagement levels correlate with better learning outcomes. Personalised and adaptive learning experiences ensure that students remain focused and motivated, leading to improved comprehension and retention.

2. **Increased Motivation:** AI can boost students' intrinsic motivation by making learning more relevant and enjoyable, driving them to engage deeply and persistently with the material.

3. **Reduced Dropout Rates:** Engaging students through personalised and interactive content can decrease the likelihood of disengagement and dropout, particularly in online and higher education settings.

4. **Development of Self-Directed Learning Skills:** AI-facilitated environments that promote engagement encourage students to take ownership of their learning. This autonomy fosters self-directed learning skills, preparing students for lifelong learning.

Practical Examples of AI Applications

1. **Duolingo:** This language learning app uses AI to personalise learning experiences and incorporate gamification, making language acquisition engaging and fun for users of all ages.

2. **ALEKS:** An adaptive learning platform that provides personalised math and science education, keeping students engaged by continuously adjusting to their learning needs.

3. **Querium's StepWise Virtual Tutor:** Uses AI to offer step-by-step assistance in STEM subjects, providing immediate feedback and hints to keep students engaged and supported as they tackle complex problems.

4. **Carnegie Learning's MATHia is an** AI-powered math learning platform that uses real-time data to provide personalised instruction and feedback, ensuring students are challenged appropriately and remain engaged.

Moving Forward

For AI to effectively enhance student engagement, educators and institutions must carefully select and implement AI tools that align with their educational objectives and student needs. Ongoing training for educators, robust data privacy measures, and equitable access to technology are essential components for leveraging AI to boost engagement successfully. As AI technologies advance, their potential to foster profoundly engaging and personalised learning experiences grows, offering promising avenues for reimagining education in the digital age.

The Future of Teacher Roles and AI Collaboration

Teachers have been pivotal in shaping education systems worldwide, traditionally focusing on direct instruction, curriculum development, and student mentoring. However, with the rapid advancement of technology, incorporating Artificial Intelligence (AI) into educational settings has begun redefining these roles. This integration offers many possibilities for enhancing teaching methodologies and personalising learning experiences, but it also raises questions about the future dynamics between teacher roles and AI collaboration.

Current Teacher Roles

Teachers today are not just educators; they are mentors, guides, and the human connection that inspires and motivates students. Their roles extend beyond imparting knowledge; they include fostering critical thinking, encouraging social development, and addressing the diverse needs of their students. Teachers adapt their teaching strategies based on the dynamic classroom environment and the unique needs of their students, a nuanced aspect that AI has yet to replicate fully.

Introduction to AI in Educational Settings

AI's introduction into education is multifaceted, ranging from intelligent tutoring systems and personalised learning platforms to administrative support and analytics. These technologies are designed to enhance the educational process by providing data-driven insights, automating routine tasks, and offering tailored learning experiences.

The promise of AI lies in its potential to complement the teacher's role, enabling educators to focus more on the interpersonal aspects of teaching and less on the administrative.

The collaboration between teachers and AI could redefine educational paradigms, making learning more adaptive and personalised. However, this collaboration also presents challenges, including ethical concerns, the digital divide, and the need for teachers to adapt to new roles that integrate technology into their teaching practices.

As we delve deeper into this topic, we must remember the historical context of educational evolution and how AI's current state plays a crucial role in shaping the future of teacher roles and AI collaboration.

Historical Context

The evolution of teaching methodologies and technology integration into education has been a gradual yet transformative process. Understanding this historical context is crucial for appreciating the potential shifts in teacher roles due to AI collaboration.

Evolution of Teaching Methodologies

- **Traditional Education**: Initially, education was characterised by rote learning and teacher-centred methodologies, where the teacher was the primary source of knowledge, and students were passive recipients. This model emphasised memorisation and standardised testing, with little room for personalised learning or critical thinking development.

- **Progressive Education Movements**: Educational reformers began advocating for student-centred approaches in the late 19th and early 20th centuries. These methods focused on the whole child, emphasising active learning, critical thinking, and the importance of adapting teaching to meet the needs of individual learners.

Progressive education sought to prepare students for life, not just to pass exams.

- **Technology Integration**: Computers and the Internet were introduced into classrooms in the late 20th and early 21st centuries, leading to more interactive and multimedia-based learning. Technology allowed for more individualised instruction and access to vast resources, significantly altering the landscape of education and teacher roles.

The Emergence of AI and Technology in Classrooms

- **Early Adoptions**: The initial phase of AI and technology in education focused on computer-assisted instruction and educational software. These tools supplement traditional teaching methods, offering math and language arts drill-and-practice exercises.

- **Interactive and Adaptive Learning Systems**: Advancements in AI led to the development of more sophisticated educational technologies, including adaptive learning platforms that personalise content to meet individual students' learning pace and style. These systems use data analytics to adjust the curriculum and provide real-time feedback to both students and teachers.

- **Beyond Instruction**: Today, AI's role in education extends beyond direct instruction. It encompasses administrative automation, predictive analytics for student performance, and tools for enhancing teacher-student interaction. AI-driven analytics can identify gaps in knowledge, predict learning outcomes, and suggest interventions, thereby supporting teachers in making data-informed decisions.

The historical progression from teacher-centred to student-centred education, coupled with increasing technology integration, sets the stage for the next frontier in education: AI collaboration. This evolution reflects a shift towards more personalised, adaptive learning experiences. It suggests a future where teacher roles are Augmented by AI, enabling educators to focus more on fostering critical thinking, creativity, and emotional intelligence.

Current State of AI Collaboration

As we dive into the current state of AI collaboration in education, let's explore how AI is already making a difference in classrooms and the experiences of both teachers and students. Integrating AI into education is not just about futuristic robots teaching classes—it's about intelligent, supportive tools that help teachers do their jobs better and make learning more enjoyable for students.

AI in the Classroom: A Helping Hand

- **Personalized Learning**: Imagine a classroom where students get a learning plan tailored just for them. AI helps make this possible. It can determine what each student knows and how they learn best, then suggest activities right for their level. This means no one gets left behind or feels bored because the work is too easy.

- **Grading and Feedback**: Teachers spend a lot of time grading assignments and tests. AI is stepping in to help with that. Now, some programs can grade multiple-choice, fill-in-the-blank questions and even help check short-written answers. This gives teachers more time to do what they love—teaching and connecting with students.

- **Support Outside the Classroom**: AI doesn't just clock out when the school day ends. Homework helpers and tutoring apps use AI to provide extra support when students are stuck on a problem at home. This way, learning doesn't have to stop at the classroom door.

The Challenges Alongside the Benefits

- **Ethics and Bias**: With all this technology, there are big questions about privacy and fairness. How do we make sure AI treats every student fairly? Sometimes, AI might make mistakes based on the data given, which could be biased. Schools and tech companies are working hard to solve these problems, ensuring AI is a fair and helpful tool for everyone.

- **Teachers and Technology**: All this new technology can overwhelm some teachers. It's a significant shift from traditional teaching methods, so training and support are essential. Teachers are learning how to team up with AI, using it to enhance their teaching, not replace it. This partnership allows teachers to spend more time doing what they do best—inspiring and guiding students.

AI: A Collaborative Partner, Not a Replacement

The heart of AI collaboration in education is the partnership between humans and machines. AI takes care of routine tasks and offers insights based on data, while teachers bring empathy, understanding, and the human touch that technology can't replicate. Together, they create a learning environment that's more inclusive, efficient, and tailored to each student's needs.

The current state of AI in education is just the beginning. As technology evolves, so will how teachers and AI collaborate, opening up new possibilities for enriching education and making learning a more personalised experience for students.

Future Predictions

Looking ahead, the collaboration between teachers and AI in education is poised to transform how we teach and learn in ways we're just beginning to imagine. Here's a glimpse into the future, where technology and human insight combine to create a learning experience that's more engaging, personalised, and inclusive than ever before.

Tailoring Education to Every Learner

- **Adaptive Learning Environments**: Imagine schools where learning adapts in real-time to the needs of each student. AI will become even better at understanding students' learning styles, strengths, and weaknesses, crafting lessons ideally suited to help each thrive. This means education can cater to everyone, making learning more effective and enjoyable.

- **Global Classrooms Without Borders**: Future AI technologies will break down geographical and language barriers, connecting students and teachers worldwide. Virtual reality (VR) and augmented reality (AR) could take this further, offering immersive learning experiences that make history, science, and the arts come alive in ways textbooks never could.

Empowering Teachers with AI Assistants

- **AI as Teachers' Co-pilot**: AI won't replace teachers but will become an invaluable assistant. It will handle administrative tasks like grading and scheduling and offer suggestions for lesson plans and classroom activities based on the latest educational research. This partnership allows teachers to focus more on the art of teaching and the personal growth of their students.

- **Real-time Feedback and Support**: AI tools will provide immediate feedback not just to students but also to teachers, helping them adjust their teaching strategies in real-time to meet the needs of their class. AI will also enhance teachers' professional development, offering personalised learning paths for educators to grow their skills and stay at the forefront of educational innovation.

Navigating Ethical and Societal Impacts

- **Ethical AI Use in Education**: As AI becomes a staple in classrooms, there will be a greater focus on ensuring its ethical use, protecting student data privacy, and preventing bias. Educational institutions, technologists, and policymakers will collaborate more closely to establish standards and regulations that safeguard students and teachers.

- **Bridging the Digital Divide**: Efforts will intensify to ensure that AI-driven education benefits everyone, not just those in well-resourced schools. Initiatives to provide access to technology in underprivileged areas will be crucial in levelling the educational playing field, ensuring that all students can benefit from AI-enhanced learning.

The future of teacher roles and AI collaboration in education is not just about adopting new technologies; it's about reimagining the learning process to make education more accessible, personalised, and effective for every student. As we move forward, the synergy between human educators and artificial intelligence will redefine the boundaries of what's possible in education, promising a future where every student has the tools and support they need to succeed.

Ethical Considerations

As the collaboration between teachers and AI in education evolves, it's essential to navigate the ethical considerations that accompany this technological advancement. Ensuring that AI serves as a force for equity, inclusivity, and fairness in education requires careful thought and action from all stakeholders involved.

Privacy and Data Security

- **Protecting Student Information**: The use of AI in education involves the collection and analysis of vast amounts of student data. Safeguarding this information is paramount to maintain trust and protect individuals' privacy. Schools and technology providers must implement robust data security measures and be transparent about how student data is used and protected.

- **Consent and Control**: Students and parents should have a say in collecting and using personal data. This includes the right to opt out of data collection or delete their information. Educators and technologists must work together to ensure that policies around consent and data control are transparent, fair, and respectful of individual rights.

Bias and Fairness

- **Addressing Algorithmic Bias**: AI systems learn from data, which means they can inherit and amplify biases in that data. To prevent discriminatory practices, AI developers must prioritise the creation of algorithms that are as unbiased as possible. This includes using diverse data sets for training AI and regularly auditing AI systems for biased outcomes.

- **Ensuring Equitable Access**: The benefits of AI in education should be available to all students, regardless of socioeconomic status, geographic location, or ability. Bridging the Digital divide is crucial to prevent exacerbating existing inequalities. This means investing in infrastructure, offering affordable technology solutions, and providing support to ensure every student can take advantage of AI-enhanced learning.

Teacher Empowerment and Student Well-being

- **Supporting Teachers**: As AI takes on more administrative tasks and offers personalised learning insights, teachers should be empowered to integrate this technology effectively into their teaching practices. Professional development and ongoing support are essential to help educators become comfortable and proficient with AI tools.

- **Fostering Human Connections**: Human interaction becomes even more critical in an AI-enhanced education system. Technology should never replace the unique insights, empathy, and inspiration that teachers provide. Instead, AI should free up teachers to engage more directly with students, fostering relationships that support emotional and social development.

Navigating these ethical considerations is a shared responsibility. By working together, educators, technologists, policymakers, and the broader community can ensure that AI enhances education in safe, equitable, and beneficial ways for all students and teachers. As we look to the future, the ethical implementation of AI in education will be just as important as the technological advancements themselves.

AI as a Collaborative Tool

The vision of AI as a collaborative tool in education is not just about integrating technology into classrooms; it's about reshaping the educational landscape to serve students better and empower teachers. AI's potential to enhance personalised learning, streamline administrative tasks, and provide insights into student performance can transform the role of teachers, allowing them to focus more on the aspects of teaching that require a human touch.

Enhancing Personalized Learning

- **Individualized Instruction Plans**: AI can analyse a student's learning history, strengths, and challenges to create a customised learning plan. This approach ensures that each student can learn at their own pace and in a way that best suits their learning style, making education more accessible and effective for everyone.

- **Real-time Adjustments**: AI systems can provide immediate feedback to students, helping them understand concepts as they learn. This immediate response loop lets students correct misunderstandings quickly and continue building on their knowledge without unnecessary delays.

Streamlining Administrative Tasks

- **Automating Routine Tasks**: AI allows teachers to dedicate more time to their students by taking over time-consuming tasks such as grading and scheduling. This shift can lead to more meaningful interactions in the classroom, with teachers having the capacity to focus on discussions, project-based learning, and individual student needs.

- **Data-Driven Insights**: AI can offer valuable insights into student performance and learning trends, helping teachers identify areas where students may need additional support. These insights can inform instructional strategies, ensuring that teaching methods are responsive to the unique dynamics of each classroom.

Supporting Teachers and Students

- **Professional Development**: AI can also support teachers' professional development by identifying skill gaps and offering personalised learning opportunities. This ensures that teachers remain at the forefront of educational practices and technological advancements.

- **Emotional and Social Learning**: AI tools can help teachers monitor students' emotional and social well-being by providing insights into engagement levels and social dynamics. This information can guide teachers in creating a supportive learning environment that fosters emotional intelligence and resilience.

AI will not replace teachers in the future but will act as a powerful ally that enhances the educational experience. This collaboration between Teachers and AI promises to create more inclusive, efficient, and personalised learning environments that cater to the diverse needs of all students. By embracing AI as a collaborative tool, educators can unlock new potential in teaching and learning, preparing students for today's challenges and tomorrow's opportunities.

The future of teacher roles and AI collaboration in education presents a landscape brimming with potential. As we have explored, integrating AI into educational settings is not merely a technological upgrade but a paradigm shift towards more personalised, efficient, and inclusive learning environments. This transformation offers a unique opportunity to enhance the educational experience for students while empowering teachers to focus on the irreplaceable human aspects of teaching.

Embracing Change

The journey ahead requires educators, technologists, policymakers, and communities to work together to navigate the challenges and opportunities presented by AI in education. By fostering a culture of innovation, continuous learning, and ethical consideration, we can ensure that the integration of AI augments the educational experience rather than diminishes the value of human interaction.

The Role of Teachers in an AI-enhanced Future

Teachers remain at the heart of the educational process. The future will likely see teachers evolving into facilitators of learning, mentors, and guides who leverage AI tools to provide personalised instruction and focus on developing critical thinking, creativity, and emotional intelligence in their students. The teacher's role becomes even more crucial in this new paradigm as they interpret AI-generated insights, foster a supportive classroom environment, and inspire students to reach their full potential.

A Collaborative Vision

The collaboration between teachers and AI is a testament to technology's incredible potential when used to complement human skills and insights. As we look forward to the future, it's clear that the most successful educational strategies will combine AI's efficiency and personalisation capabilities with teachers' empathy, creativity, and passion. Together, AI and educators can create a future where learning is more accessible, engaging, and tailored to the needs of every student.

In conclusion, the future of teacher roles and AI collaboration in education is not just about adopting new technologies; it's about rethinking how we educate, ensuring that every student has the opportunity to succeed in an increasingly complex world. By embracing this collaborative approach, we can unlock a future of limitless educational possibilities.

Scaling Quality Education through AI

The Potential of AI in Education

So, searching for quality education becomes one of the most severe challenges and opportunities. As modernity is a world of knowledge, the ability to provide scalable, accessible, and quality education is not a matter of education itself but also a socio-economic developmental need.

However, with the burgeoning of globally diverse learner populations, these traditional models often need help to scale or be adaptive enough. That is where Artificial Intelligence (AI) offers disruptive solutions poised to remake the educational landscape.

Thus, artificial intelligence has an unparalleled capacity for data processing, pattern recognition, and decision-making understanding and can give the educational world a facelift. AI can offer scalable solutions that would fit the learner's needs for Learning experiences that are more interesting, engaging, effective, and personalised. The advent of AI may change all this, and educators will have the choice of moving out of traditional borders to reach out with quality education to even the remotest and most underprivileged communities.

Such an AI-based educational tool will be able to find learning gaps with greater accuracy and help supply suitable content for individual students, making the educational process more inclusive and fairer. These technologies help automate administrative tasks, ensuring educators spend more time teaching and less on bureaucratic activities.

The promise of AI in education is excellent, from personalised learning and grading automation to real-time feedback, dynamic and interactive content, and even the ability to create virtual learning environments. The innovations will possess a quality that will make the learning process attractive, accessible, and effective.

However, it is not free of challenges: privacy, data security, ethical considerations, and the digital divide must be bridged, ensuring that AI is a tool for empowerment, not exclusion.

In conclusion, AI's potential in education is vast and varied. At the brink of this technological revolution, it is thus imperative that one approaches the integration of AI into education with optimism and caution, seeing to it that it does play out as a force for good: scaling quality education to every corner of the globe.

Challenges in Scaling Quality Education

They pose a complex challenge that must be tackled comprehensively to scale quality education globally equitably and assure each learner of high-quality learning experiences. All these challenges could be roughly categorised into three main categories: disparities of educational access, poor quality and relevancy of the delivered educational content, and teacher training and support.

Access Disparities

These are some of the main barriers to quality education: Equitable access is a very complex area that includes geographical and socio-economic factors, differences in terms of technological access, and digital resources. Eventually, students in these far-off or less-favoured areas need more access to quality educational materials and qualified teachers. The digital divide continues perpetuating since many learners need more gadgets or internet connectivity, which otherwise could have allowed them to access online resources or even take advantage of available digital learning platforms.

Quality and Relevance of Content

The second is ensuring the quality and relevance of educational content. In most cases, school curricula have yet to keep pace with an evolving world, leaving a gap between what students are taught and what is required to find their place in the modern workforce. This void tends to imply a need for dynamic, adaptable content that can be updated in real-time to reflect the latest knowledge and industry demands.

Teacher Training and Support

Teachers are the cradle of the learning ecosystem. Still, most face challenges that limit correct training, especially the new technologies they should use to impact and change the face of learning. Critical shortages of qualified teachers are also witnessed in most regions, straining the capacity to over-provide quality education to all learners. Teachers often need support mechanisms to burn out or move on, compounding the challenge of quality education delivery at scale.

Such challenges necessitate the search for innovative solutions that bridge the access gap and guarantee the relevance and quality of content required for education and the teacher's critical role. The paper will also conclude by discussing how AI offers promising avenues for addressing these issues, from personalised learning platforms that adopt the needs of individual students to AI-driven content delivery tools and AI administrative assistants for teachers.

Artificial intelligence can put such into perspective, which will help stakeholders solve these challenges that have posed significant hurdles to scalable quality education accessible to learners worldwide.

AI Solutions for Scaling Quality Education

AI promises many solutions to overcome this barrier to scaling quality education. If leveraged, AI in this problem will result in an educational system that is adaptive, efficient, and more accessible to the student population, therefore allowing for the personalised learning experiences of every student.

Personalised Learning Experiences

AI-powered personalised learning platforms use data analytic techniques and machine learning algorithms to optimise educational content in sync with an individual student's learning style, preference, and performance. These platforms can switch their support in real-time and give adapted resources and learning paths according to the pace and style of different individual learners. This increases engagement and motivation, allowing them to understand and grasp complex problems, leading to improved outcomes.

Adaptive learning technologies: These are systems of AI that analyse performance data strengths and weaknesses of the learning patterns, then adapt their curriculum in response to such analysis.

Interactive content with ease: AI can generate even interactive content, such as simulation, gaming, quizzing, etc., which makes learning interactive and fun.

Automated Grading and Feedback Systems

It will thus help save time by instantly grading assignments and automatically grading exams, giving immediate feedback to the student. This would reduce a teacher's work, giving more time for teaching and giving students timely insights into their progress and areas of improvement when required.

Instant feedback mechanisms: The AI tools ensure instant feedback by offering instant real-time corrections and instantaneously providing suggestions, making learning more iterative and adaptive.

Personalised Feedback: More than grading, AI systems can give personalised feedback that will help the student understand where they went wrong and thus benefit in learning much better.

AI-driven Content Creation and Curation

Artificial intelligence can help generate and curate such content, ensuring it is updated and relevant. Artificial intelligence algorithms can process a massive volume of data, indicating trends and gaps within educational content; they recommend what needs updating and new content so that the curriculum remains at pace with the present knowledge and industrial requirements.

New findings and the latest information are updated dynamically, and the educational resources are automatically updated with the latest methods and discoveries.

Tailoring of content: Development of customised learning material that includes current events,
student interests, and real-world applications.

Virtual Teachers and Assistants

AI-powered virtual teachers and assistants are very useful for students in terms of explanations, answering questions, and learning guidance when the student is outside the four walls of traditional classes. These AI assistants are available to students at any time during the day and night, providing assistance and giving them resources right at the moment that the student needs, thus enhancing continuity and availability in learning.

Round-the-clock Assistance: Students can engage with educational content and receive support anytime.

Scalable Support: Virtual assistants can support many students at a time.

These AI solutions represent a transformative approach toward scaling quality education, attuned to dealing with the core challenges in access, engagement, and personalised learning. Therefore, if combined, learning with such technologies can allow educational systems to be included increasingly yet effectively and adaptively for students worldwide.

Integrating Graphical Analysis, Generation, Image Classification, and Object Detection in Education

It integrates the highest-speed technologies of image classification and object detection with graphical analysis and generation, revolutionising educational methodologies and opening new dimensions to establish profound, immersive, interactive, and personalised learning experiences across domains.

These technologies harness the power of visual data to better students' comprehension, engagement, and analytic skills. They offer learners and their tutors unlimited opportunities to investigate and make meaning of complex concepts through the visualisation medium.

Graphical Analysis and Generation This makes graphical analysis and generation an essentially sought-after element in education, one whose role it serves: making abstract visualisation of concepts and data accessible to learners at all levels. Other technologies allow educators to dynamically show mathematical equations, scientific phenomena, and statistics in visual, dynamic formats through dynamic graphing software, data visualisation tools, and virtual simulations.

For example, in physics or biology, the simulation and visualisation of complex processes could enable students to experiment with more than one variable simultaneously and visualise the result in real time, bringing theory closer to practical application.

Such technologies also empower students to create and design visual content, which develops creativity, critical thinking, and problem-solving skills. Students can design graphs, charts, and models to investigate data patterns, the relationship between variables, and the presentation of findings in a much more visual and presentable way.

Image Classification and Object Detection Advancements in artificial intelligence (AI) and machine learning that have image classification and object detection capabilities find educational applications.

These listed technologies make it possible to recognise and categorise objects in pictures, and they may be applied to tasks ranging from automated grading of visual assignments to creating interactive materials.

Applied to image classification in environmental science, geography, or biology, it will allow the identification of plant species, geological formations, or animal types from images; hence, it becomes a handy tool in field studies or research projects.

Beyond this, object detection could also find applications in safety training simulations, historical artefact recognition, or even in developing augmented reality (AR) experiences for educational purposes.

Both technologies could be integrated into educational software and apps to build engaging, student-centred learning environments that improve learners' ability to explore and self-discover new concepts.

Bridging the Gap between Theory and Application This addition to learning dramatically improves the combination of graphical analysis, image generation, image classification, and object detection, preparing students well for the demands of technology in the future workforce.

This involves students' practical application of theoretical knowledge, teaching a deeper understanding of the subject matter and applying learning in real-life situations.

For example, in computer science and engineering education, students may engage in projects such as developing artificial intelligence models for classifying images and detecting objects, putting those approaches into practice with coding and algorithms.

Like the design courses, they have been able to present their contribution to the art and design of education and technology through analysis of art styles, patterns, and techniques, which bring out new light and perspective in the creative process.

Challenges and Ethical Considerations: While there is great potential for these technologies in the education sector, there are also some challenges, from the required adequate infrastructure to the digital literacy of educators and students to clear data privacy and ethical use of AI.

Ensuring equal access to such tools is one of the considerations required to facilitate and assure their successful integration, in addition to addressing the moral implications of using them within educational contexts.

The integration of computerised graphical analysis and generation power with technologies of image classification and object detection truly blazes a trail for a new paradigm in education, bringing along innovative teaching and learning.

Thus, educators are better placed to develop more attractive, practical, and personalised learning experiences as enabled by these visualisation tools toward higher academic achievement, offering students skills to survive and thrive in an increasingly sophisticated technological environment.

Both these technologies will improve, and their integration into the education framework holds a vital reflective role concerning the future of education.

Following the inclusion of graphical analysis, generation, image classification, and object detection into the school curriculum, it is herewith stated that the detailed roles that these technologies are now playing have become very crucial towards the revolution of learning and learning experiences, increasing learner engagement in classes, and helping the students acquire necessary skills and competencies indispensable in the 21st century.

These visual technologies could only synergise with educational practices to open up new areas of understanding complex concepts, research, and creativity building in different disciplines.

An image that depicts a classroom uniquely designed for teaching and demonstrating AI technologies, including image generation, image classification, and object detection. Each classroom zone is tailored to explore

one of these technologies, providing an immersive and interactive learning experience.

Deepening Understanding with Advanced Visualization

Advanced visualisation techniques, such as graphical analysis and generation tools, allow the exploration of otherwise tricky concepts. Even in certain subjects, such as chemistry, three-dimensional molecular modelling software will enable students to seek illustrative details of chemical structures, allowing more intuitive ways to understand spatial relationships and molecular interactions.

For instance, in geography, dynamic earth mapping tools make it possible to represent change on land due to climatic effects over a long time, bringing such abstract concepts as global warming to life.

Enhancing Interactive Learning through Image Classification AI-powered image classification technologies can transform traditionally dull, static, monologue-like learning activities into interactive, engaging dialogues.

In language learning, for example, image classification could be deployed in developing applications whose goal is to allow learners to associate words with images that convey their context of applicability, enhancing their ability to capture and remember words.

This tool may equally be applied in special education, whereby image-based means of communication assist the learner with problems in speech and language to provide alternative means through which such learners may express themselves and communicate with their environment.

Facilitating Research and Exploration with Object Detection

Object detection technology unlocks new possibilities for student-driven research and exploration in ways never before possible. Be it the study of forests, their health, deforestation, urban development, or wildlife migrations, satellite imagery or drone footage can easily be analysed with the help of object detection. This learning approach to data analysis enhances the learning outcomes, providing students with a fuller understanding of the matter so that they can responsibly engage with issues of being global citizens.

Bridging Practical Skills with Theoretical Knowledge

Object detection technology allows for the integration of practical skills such as graphical analysis, image classification, and object detection into project-based learning initiatives. Students can apply these skills in research projects, such as designing and deploying AI models for autonomous vehicles, where they collaboratively apply physics, mathematics, and computer science knowledge. This approach not only solidifies theoretical concepts but also develops critical teamwork, innovation, and technical proficiency skills, making students feel more prepared and competent.

This approach allows students to take theoretical concepts learned from reading their textbooks and solidify them through experience while developing critical teamwork, innovation, and technical proficiency skills.

Preparing for the Future Workforce

Educators who integrate object detection technology into their curriculum are not just teaching; they prepare their students for the future workforce. As more industries seek data visualization, image analysis, or AI skills for healthcare, biotech, finance, or city planning, these students will be well-equipped and ready to meet these demands, making educators and policymakers feel more proactive and forward-thinking.

These will provide students with value-added capabilities that motivate them to pursue higher studies and careers in STEM and contribute to the highly skilled, innovative workforce.

Addressing Challenges and Moving Forward Therefore, solving the direct challenges linked with accessibility, digital literacy, and ethical considerations is a precondition toward realising the full potential role of these technologies in education.

It will, therefore, be necessary to put in place all-round training for educators to ensure that there will be access to technology in an all-inclusive way, with discussions on the use of AI in the education stage.

Collaboration among educators, technologists, and policymakers will encourage cutting-edge, inclusive educational technologies.

In education, graphical analysis, generation, image classification, and object detection are all technologies whose detailed exploration within this domain underlines their transformational potential for enriching learning experiences, driving creativity, and better-preparing students for upcoming challenges.

As these changes continue to advance and impact education, integrating such visual technologies into education becomes central to innovative, engaging, and effective practices in 21st-century education.

CHAPTER 6

AI Technologies and Chatbots in Education

The birth of the digital age is revolutionising the educational landscape, with technology positioning itself front and centre to mould the learning experiences of tomorrow. Therefore, Chatbots are among the many technological advancements at play and are making learning support redefine enhancement.

Bots, chatbots, or conversational agents refer to programs armed with AI that simulate human-like interaction with the user in dispensing support and service-based information delivery, majorly through text and, to a lesser extent, voice communication. Their integration in educational settings thus holds a promise for facilitating accessible, personalised, and efficient learner experiences.

Benefits and Applications in Learning Environments
Chatbots in education take on numerous roles, from virtual tutors to administrative assistants. One of the great benefits of employing chatbots in the education sector is providing a one-on-one learning experience.

Such chatbots can improve the response in their referential materials and adjust them according to individual learning needs and the way students learn, allowing them to achieve more interactivity and understanding of learning materials.

Further, the 24/7 answered questions chatbots even help students get explanations or assistance for complicated topics when offline class hours are active. Some of the 24/7 availability provides help to students at any time of need, thus ensuring continuity in learning and reducing the barriers to time and space.

Other areas of chatbot integration include those mentioned above in enrolment, coursework timetable, and on-campus events and services information that deals with administration. These reduce the administrative workload on the staff and, therefore, increase efficiency in the administration of resources available to the students.

Challenges and Considerations
Despite their potential, integrating chatbots in learning environments takes time and effort. Ensuring the accuracy and relevance of chatbot responses is paramount to avoid Disse refraining from incorrect information. This requires ongoing development and refinement of chatbot algorithms and databases.

Privacy and security concerns also come to the forefront, mainly when collecting and analysing sensitive student data. Implementing robust data protection measures and transparent privacy policies is essential to safeguard user information.

Furthermore, the effectiveness of chatbots in education depends on their ability to understand and respond to a wide range of queries and expressions. Developing chatbots that can accurately interpret natural language and provide contextually appropriate responses is a complex task that requires significant resources and expertise.

Future Directions

In the future, with advancements in AI technology, chatbots' abilities will expand, and new applications will be established for their skills in education. This may include more advanced NLP algorithms that would make chatbots understand and respond more naturally and accurately to the user. The idea is also that voice recognition technology can be easily incorporated into chatbots, mainly catering to physically disabled or very young learners.

An attractive area to investigate would be how chatbots, in further development, could be used to support these collaborative learning experiences through further peer interaction. Chatbots would help improve the learning environment, allowing community building through better student communication and collaboration.

Chatbots represent a monumental leap forward in learning and educational support across all settings. Their capacity to deliver personalized, accessible, and ultimately beneficial assistance positions them as transformative elements in the academic experience. Their successful integration will demand meticulous attention to detail and deep respect for private and natural language understanding.

The evolution of technology ensures that chatbots will play an undeniable role in education. A future brimming with possibilities awaits, not just for learners, but also for educators, as chatbots continue to revolutionize the educational landscape.

Technical Aspects of Developing Educational Chatbots

Exploring the technical aspects of developing educational chatbots involves understanding the foundational technologies, design principles, and methodologies that underpin their creation and effective deployment in learning environments.

This segment delves into the crucial components of chatbot development, including natural language processing (NLP), machine learning, user interface design, and integration with educational content and systems.

Natural Language Processing (NLP) is at the heart of any chatbot. It is a branch of artificial intelligence that enables machines to understand, interpret, and respond to human language. Educational chatbots leverage NLP to process and comprehend students' queries and comments, allowing meaningful and contextually relevant interactions. Machine learning algorithms further enhance a chatbot's capabilities, enabling it to learn from interactions and improve its responses over time. These technologies ensure that chatbots can adapt to learners' diverse linguistic styles and educational needs.

- **Key Components**:
    - **Tokenization**: For easier processing, breaking down text into manageable pieces, such as words or phrases.
    - **Sentiment Analysis**: Assessing the emotional tone behind a user's message to tailor responses accordingly.
    - **Intent Recognition**: Identifying the purpose of a user's message to generate the most appropriate response.

User Interface Design

The effectiveness of an educational chatbot also heavily relies on its user interface (UI) design. A well-designed UI ensures that interactions with the chatbot are intuitive, engaging, and conducive to learning. This includes considerations for how the chatbot presents text-based content, handles voice interactions (if applicable), and guides users through educational materials and activities. Simplicity and clarity are paramount, ensuring that users of all ages and technical proficiencies can interact with the chatbot without confusion.

Integration with Educational Content and Systems

To be truly effective, educational chatbots must be seamlessly integrated with existing educational content and learning management systems (LMS). This integration enables chatbots to access various educational materials and resources, from textbooks and articles to videos and interactive modules, and recommend these resources to students based on their learning needs. Additionally, integrating chatbots with LMS allows tracking student progress and performance, enabling more personalised and data-driven educational support.

- **Integration Challenges**:
    - **Data Interoperability**: Ensuring chatbots can effectively communicate with and retrieve data from various educational databases and platforms.
    - **Content Customization**: Adapting educational content to be easily accessible and understandable in a conversational format.

Ethical and Privacy Considerations

Developing educational chatbots also entails navigating ethical and privacy considerations, particularly regarding handling student data. Developers must implement robust data protection measures and ensure compliance with educational privacy laws, such as the Family Educational Rights and Privacy Act (FERPA) in the United States. Transparency with users about data collection, usage, and storage practices is crucial to maintaining trust and safeguarding privacy.

Strategies for Implementing Chatbots in Diverse Educational Settings

Discussing strategies for implementing chatbots in diverse educational settings involves considering different learning environments' varying needs, resources, and goals. This includes traditional classrooms, online learning platforms, and informal learning spaces. Effective implementation requires a thoughtful approach that addresses technical infrastructure, pedagogical integration, and stakeholder engagement.

Assessing Needs and Setting Objectives

The development of educational chatbots is a complex, multidisciplinary endeavour that requires expertise in AI, software engineering, user experience design, and academic theory. Developers can create compelling, engaging, and secure chatbots that enhance the learning experience by addressing the technical challenges and ethical considerations involved. As these technologies evolve, the potential for educational chatbots to support and transform learning is boundless.

The first step in implementing chatbots in educational settings is to assess the specific needs of the learners and the institution. This assessment should identify the gaps and challenges in the current educational delivery that chatbots could address, such as providing 24/7 support, supplementing teacher instruction, or facilitating administrative tasks. Setting clear objectives for what the chatbot is expected to achieve is crucial for guiding its development and deployment.

- **Needs Assessment**: Understand the learners' needs, teachers' challenges, and administrative bottlenecks.
- **Objective Setting**: Define clear, measurable goals for the chatbot, such as improving student engagement, enhancing learning outcomes, or reducing administrative workload.

Designing for Inclusivity and Accessibility

Inclusivity and accessibility should be core considerations in chatbot design. This ensures that the technology supports a wide range of learners, including those with disabilities or those who may not have prior experience with chatbots. Design choices should consider diverse learning styles, languages, and cultural contexts to create an engaging and supportive learning environment for all students.

- **Multilingual Support**: Implementing language options to cater to non-native speakers and linguistic diversity.

- **Accessibility Features**: Designing chatbots to be accessible to users with disabilities, such as text-to-speech for visually impaired learners.

Integrating with Pedagogical Approaches

Chatbots should be integrated into the broader pedagogical framework, complementing existing teaching methodologies and enhancing the learning experience rather than replacing traditional teaching methods. This integration involves aligning chatbot interactions with learning objectives, curriculum standards, and assessment methods.

- **Curriculum Alignment**: Ensuring chatbot content and activities are aligned with curriculum goals and learning outcomes.

- **Blended Learning Integration**: Combining chatbot interactions with classroom activities, online resources, and hands-on learning experiences.

Technical Implementation and Support

The technical implementation of chatbots requires careful planning to ensure compatibility with existing educational technologies and infrastructure. This includes selecting the right platform for the chatbot, ensuring data security and privacy, and providing ongoing technical support for users.

- **Platform Selection**: Choosing a chatbot platform that integrates seamlessly with existing LMS and educational tools.

- **Data Security**: Implementing robust data protection measures to safeguard student information.

Continuous Evaluation and Improvement

Once deployed, the effectiveness of educational chatbots should be continuously evaluated against the set objectives. Feedback from students, teachers, and administrators should be collected to inform iterative improvements, ensuring the chatbot remains relevant and effective over time.

- **Feedback Mechanisms**: Establishing channels for users to provide feedback on their chatbot experiences.
- **Performance Metrics**: Monitoring usage data and learning outcomes to assess the chatbot's impact and identify areas for enhancement.

Implementing chatbots in diverse educational settings requires a strategic approach that considers each learning environment's unique needs and contexts. By prioritising inclusivity, pedagogical integration, and continuous improvement, academic institutions can leverage chatbots to enhance learning experiences, support teachers, and streamline administrative processes.

As educational technologies continue to evolve, chatbots represent a flexible and innovative tool for enriching education across various settings.

Diving into case studies of chatbot implementation in education provides valuable insights into the practical applications, benefits, and challenges of using these technologies in real-world settings.

By examining specific examples, we can better understand how chatbots enhance learning experiences, support students and educators, and address the unique needs of different educational environments.

Case Studies of Chatbot Implementation in Education

Case Study 1: University Virtual Assistant

Background: A prominent university implemented a chatbot named "CampusHelper" to assist students in navigating campus life, from academic inquiries to administrative tasks.

Implementation: CampusHelper was integrated into the university's online portal and mobile app, offering 24/7 support to students. It was designed to answer questions on course schedules, enrolment processes, campus events, and student services.

Outcomes: The chatbot significantly reduced the administrative workload on staff, allowing them to focus on more complex student support tasks. Student satisfaction with administrative processes increased, as they could get instant answers to their queries anytime. The chatbot also helped new students acclimate more quickly to campus life.

Challenges: Ensuring the chatbot provided accurate and up-to-date information required continuous updates to its knowledge base, especially regarding course schedules and campus events.

Case Study 2: High School Tutoring Bot

Background: A high school introduced a chatbot, "StudyBuddy," to provide additional tutoring support in mathematics and science subjects after school hours.

Implementation: StudyBuddy was accessible via a web-based platform and integrated with the school's learning management system. It offered step-by-step explanations for common problems, interactive quizzes, and personalised learning recommendations based on student performance.

Outcomes: StudyBuddy students reported improved understanding of complex concepts and felt more confident in their coursework. The chatbot also allowed teachers to identify common areas of difficulty among students, informing targeted classroom instruction.

Challenges: Some students sometimes found the chatbot's explanations too generic, indicating a need for more personalised and in-depth tutoring capabilities.

Case Study 3: Language Learning Companion

Background: An online language learning platform launched a chatbot, "LingoPal," to enhance its users' language practice and cultural learning.

Implementation: LingoPal offered conversational practice in multiple languages, using natural language processing to correct grammar and pronunciation errors. It also provided cultural insights and idiomatic expressions to enrich learning.

Outcomes: LingoPal users experienced more engaging and interactive language learning, with many reporting faster progress in conversational skills. The chatbot's instant feedback and corrections were particularly valued for independent learning.

Challenges: Developing a chatbot capable of accurately recognising and correcting pronunciation in multiple languages required advanced AI capabilities and significant investment.

These case studies illustrate the diverse applications of chatbots in education, from administrative support and tutoring to language learning. While chatbots have shown significant potential in enhancing learning experiences and operational efficiency, their implementation comes with challenges such as maintaining accuracy, ensuring personalisation, and developing advanced technical capabilities.

Continuous evaluation and improvement are crucial for maximising chatbots' benefits in educational settings. As AI technology advances, chatbots' role in education will likely grow, offering new opportunities for innovation in learning and support.

Ethical Considerations in Educational Chatbots

Reviewing the ethical considerations in deploying chatbots in education is paramount to ensuring these technologies serve as beneficial tools without compromising privacy, equity, or the quality of education. This exploration will address critical ethical issues, including data privacy, bias and fairness, transparency, and the potential impact on the teacher-student relationship.

Data Privacy and Security

One of the foremost ethical concerns with using chatbots in education revolves around handling sensitive student data. Chatbots often collect and analyse vast amounts of personal information to personalise learning experiences and improve functionality. Ensuring the privacy and security of this data is crucial to protect students from potential breaches and misuse.

- **Measures**: To safeguard privacy, robust data encryption, strict data protection regulations (such as GDPR), and user control over data are essential.

Bias and Fairness

AI and machine learning models, including those powering chatbots, can inadvertently perpetuate and amplify biases in their training data. This can lead to unfair or discriminatory responses that affect students differently based on their background, culture, or learning abilities.

- **Addressing Bias**: Strategies to mitigate these issues include regularly auditing chatbot algorithms for bias, using diverse datasets for training, and incorporating fairness metrics.

Transparency and Accountability

Transparency about how chatbots function, the data they collect, and how they make decisions is vital to maintaining trust among users. Stakeholders should be informed about chatbots' capabilities and limitations to set realistic expectations and ensure accountability for their performance.

- **Implementation**: Providing clear user agreements, explaining chatbot responses, and establishing oversight mechanisms can enhance transparency and accountability.

Impact on Teacher-Student Relationship

While chatbots can offer valuable support and augment learning, there is a concern that overreliance on these tools could diminish the importance of human interaction in education. The teacher-student relationship plays a critical role in motivation, emotional support, and the development of critical thinking skills.

- **Balancing Technology and Human Interaction**: It's essential to position chatbots as complementary tools that support, rather than replace, the valuable human elements of teaching and learning. Ensuring that chatbots facilitate rather than hinder teacher-student interactions is critical.

Ensuring Equitable Access

The deployment of chatbots in education must also consider equitable access to these technologies. Differences in technological infrastructure, internet access, and digital literacy can lead to disparities in the benefits received from educational chatbots.

- **Promoting Equity**: Developing low-bandwidth versions of chatbots, ensuring compatibility with various devices, and providing training for students and teachers can help bridge the digital divide.

Ethical considerations in deploying educational chatbots are critical to their success and acceptance. By addressing concerns related to data privacy, bias, transparency, the teacher-student relationship, and equitable access, educators and technologists can ensure that chatbots serve as ethical, effective, and inclusive tools in education.

As chatbots evolve, ongoing dialogue and evaluation of these ethical dimensions will be essential to harness their potential responsibly.

Practical Steps for Ethical Implementation of Educational Chatbots

Discussing practical steps for implementing chatbots ethically in education involves a series of actions and considerations to ensure that these technological tools enhance the learning experience without compromising ethical standards or exacerbating existing inequalities. This approach emphasises transparency, inclusivity, privacy, and the complementary role of chatbots to human instruction.

Step 1: Conduct a Thorough Needs Assessment

Before implementing chatbots, it's crucial to understand the specific needs of the educational environment, including the students, teachers, and administrative staff. This assessment should identify the areas where chatbots can provide the most value, such as personalised learning support or administrative task automation, while also considering the potential ethical implications.

- **Action**: Engage with stakeholders through surveys, interviews, and focus groups to gather insights on their needs and concerns.

Step 2: Ensure Data Privacy and Security

Protecting the privacy and security of student data is paramount. Implementing chatbots must involve strict adherence to data protection laws and ethical guidelines, ensuring that all collected data is used responsibly and securely.

- **Action**: Use encryption for data storage and transmission, obtain user consent for data collection, and regularly review compliance with relevant data protection regulations.

Step 3: Address Bias and Ensure Fairness

To prevent the perpetuation of bias through chatbots, developers must use diverse and representative datasets in training AI models. Regular audits for bias and fairness should also be conducted to identify and correct any issues.

- **Action**: Incorporate diverse perspectives in the development team, conduct bias audits, and iteratively refine chatbot responses based on feedback.

Step 4: Maintain Transparency and Accountability

Transparency about how chatbots operate, the scope of their capabilities, and how they handle data is essential for building user trust. Clear communication about these aspects ensures stakeholders have realistic expectations and understand the chatbot's role in the educational process.

- **Action**: Provide accessible user guides, disclose data usage policies, and establish a feedback mechanism for users to report issues or concerns.

Step 5: Complement, Not Replace, Human Interaction

Chatbots should be integrated into the educational process as tools that complement and support human teaching and learning, not replacements. Ensuring that chatbots enhance, rather than diminish, the teacher-student relationship is crucial for their ethical implementation.

- **Action**: Design chatbot interactions that encourage critical thinking and creativity and ensure that human support is available for complex or sensitive issues.

Step 6: Promote Equitable Access

Implementations must consider accessibility and inclusivity from the outset to ensure that the benefits of chatbots are accessible to all students, including those from underrepresented or disadvantaged backgrounds.

- **Action**: Develop chatbots that are accessible on multiple platforms and devices, offer multilingual support, and provide training for students and teachers to use the technology effectively.

Step 7: Continuous Evaluation and Improvement

The ethical implementation of chatbots requires ongoing evaluation to assess their impact on learning outcomes, student engagement, and ethical considerations. This process should inform continuous improvements to chatbot functionality and deployment strategies.

- **Action**: Implement monitoring and evaluation frameworks to assess chatbot effectiveness, collect stakeholder feedback, and make iterative improvements based on findings.

Implementing chatbots in education ethically requires a multifaceted approach prioritising all stakeholders' well-being, privacy, and needs. By following these practical steps, educational institutions can leverage chatbots' benefits to enhance learning experiences while adhering to ethical standards and promoting equity and inclusion.

Virtual Reality (VR) and Augmented Reality (AR) in Education

Virtual Reality (VR) and Augmented Reality (AR) represent two of the most exciting technological advancements in recent years, potentially revolutionising how educational content is delivered and experienced. This book explores the integration of VR and AR into educational settings, examining their benefits, challenges, applications, and prospects.

Virtual Reality (VR) immerses users in a wholly digital environment, while Augmented Reality (AR) overlays digital information into the real world. In educational contexts, these technologies offer immersive and interactive experiences that can enhance learning outcomes, engagement, and motivation across various subjects and age groups.

Benefits of VR and AR in Education

Enhanced Engagement and Immersion

VR and AR can transform learning from a passive to an active experience, engaging students in a way traditional methods cannot. By immersing learners in the subject matter, these technologies foster a deeper understanding and retention of information.

Accessible Experiential Learning

VR and AR enable experiential learning opportunities that might be impractical or impossible in the real world due to logistical, safety, or financial constraints. Students can explore historical sites, conduct complex scientific experiments, or practice medical procedures in a controlled, risk-free environment.

Personalised Learning

These technologies can be tailored to meet individual learning styles and needs, offering personalised pathways through educational content. AR and VR applications can adjust to a learner's pace and provide immediate feedback, enhancing the learning experience.

Applications of VR and AR in Education

Science and Mathematics

VR and AR can visualise complex scientific concepts and mathematical theories, making abstract concepts tangible. Students can interact with 3D models of molecules, human anatomy, or mathematical shapes, improving their understanding and engagement.

History and Culture

Virtual tours of historical sites, museums, and cultural landmarks allow students to explore and learn about different eras and societies firsthand, fostering a greater appreciation and understanding of history and cultural diversity.

Language Learning

Language learning benefits from AR and VR through immersive experiences that simulate real-life conversations and cultural contexts, offering a more natural and engaging way to learn new languages.

Special Education

VR and AR offer unique advantages for special education. They provide customisable experiences that cater to individual learning challenges. These technologies can help develop social, fine motor, and cognitive skills in a supportive environment.

Challenges and Considerations

While VR and AR hold great promise for education, their implementation comes with challenges. Significant considerations include the high cost of technology, the need for robust infrastructure, potential health concerns (such as motion sickness in VR), and ensuring equitable access. Additionally, educators require training to integrate these technologies effectively into their teaching practices.

Future Prospects

The future of VR and AR in education is bright, with ongoing technological advancements making these tools more accessible and practical. Emerging trends include the integration of artificial intelligence to create more personalised learning experiences, developing collaborative VR and AR environments for group learning, and expanding content across various educational disciplines.

VR and AR have the potential to fundamentally transform the educational landscape by providing immersive, interactive, and personalised learning experiences. As these technologies evolve and become more integrated into educational settings, they promise to enhance academic outcomes and prepare students for a future in which digital and physical realities are increasingly intertwined.

Exploring the technical requirements for implementing Virtual Reality (VR) and Augmented Reality (AR)

Exploring the technical requirements for implementing Virtual Reality (VR) and Augmented Reality (AR) in educational settings involves understanding the necessary hardware, software, and infrastructure to support these technologies effectively. This analysis will provide insight into the foundational elements needed to integrate VR and AR into classrooms, ensuring a seamless and impactful learning experience.

Hardware Requirements

VR Headsets and Input Devices

For VR, headsets are the primary hardware, ranging from high-end models requiring connection to a PC to standalone devices and more affordable options that work with smartphones. Input devices such as controllers, gloves, or motion sensors are essential for interacting within the virtual environment.

- **High-End VR Headsets**: Offer the best immersive experience but require powerful PCs.
- **Standalone VR Headsets**: Balance performance and convenience, operating without external hardware.
- **Mobile VR Headsets**: Provide a cost-effective VR entry point, using smartphones to power the experience.

AR Devices

AR implementations can use smartphones and tablets, which are more commonly available and can overlay digital information onto the real-world view through their cameras and screens. Specialised AR glasses offer a more immersive experience by projecting digital images directly into the user's field of vision.

- **Smartphones and Tablets**: Accessible and versatile tools for AR experiences.
- **AR Glasses**: Offer hands-free, immersive AR at a higher cost and with limited availability.

Software Requirements

The software for VR and AR includes the operating systems, applications, and development platforms necessary to create and run educational content. Compatibility with academic standards and learning management systems (LMS) is also crucial.

- **Content Creation Tools**: Software like Unity or Unreal Engine allows the development of custom VR and AR educational experiences.
- **Educational Applications**: Pre-built applications covering various subjects and grade levels must be evaluated for educational relevance and engagement.
- **Integration with LMS**: Ensuring VR and AR content can track and report on student progress within existing LMS platforms.

Infrastructure and Connectivity

Adequate infrastructure, including high-speed internet connectivity and compatible devices, is essential for downloading content and enabling interactive, multi-user experiences. For high-end VR, sufficient physical space is necessary to accommodate movement safely.

- **High-speed Internet**: Necessary for downloading VR and AR content and supporting interactive online experiences.

- **Device Compatibility and Availability**: Ensuring that devices meet the minimum specifications for running VR and AR software and that there are enough devices for student use.

- **Physical Space**: A safe, open area is needed, especially for VR, to allow free movement without risk of injury or damage to equipment.

Training and Support

Educators must receive adequate training on using VR and AR technologies, including understanding best practices for integration into curricula and troubleshooting technical issues. Ongoing technical support is also crucial to address hardware or software problems.

- **Professional Development**: Training programs for teachers to effectively incorporate VR and AR into their teaching strategies.

- **Technical Support**: A support system to quickly resolve hardware and software issues to minimise disruptions to learning.

The successful implementation of VR and AR in education requires careful consideration of hardware, software, infrastructure, and support needs. While integrating these technologies presents challenges, including costs and the need for training, the potential benefits for enhancing learning experiences are significant. As VR and AR technologies become more accessible and their educational applications more developed, schools will be better positioned to leverage these immersive tools to support innovative and effective teaching and learning practices.

Case studies of successful VR and AR applications in education.

Delving into case studies of successful Virtual Reality (VR) and Augmented Reality (AR) applications in education provides concrete examples of how these technologies are being used to enhance learning and teaching experiences across various disciplines and age groups. These case studies illustrate the potential of VR and AR to transform traditional educational paradigms, offering insights into their practical implementation and impact.

Case Study 1: VR Field Trips

Background: A middle school implemented VR field trips to provide students with immersive learning experiences previously inaccessible due to geographical or financial constraints.

Implementation: Using VR headsets, students embarked on guided tours of historical sites, natural wonders, and even extraterrestrial environments. The program integrated the social studies and science curricula, enhancing lessons with vivid, experiential learning.

Outcomes: Students demonstrated increased engagement and retention of the material. Teachers noted a significant rise in student participation and enthusiasm for previously more challenging subjects to bring to life through traditional teaching methods.

Challenges: Initial challenges included the cost of VR equipment and the need for teacher training on effectively integrating VR experiences into their lesson plans.

Case Study 2: AR for Anatomy Education

Background: A university's medical school used AR to teach human anatomy, addressing the limitations of textbook diagrams and cadaver dissections.

Implementation: AR applications let students visualise and interact with 3D human body models, layering anatomical structures in real space. This approach facilitated a deeper understanding of complex anatomical relationships and variations.

Outcomes: Students reported a better grasp of anatomy, and the ability to visualise structures in three dimensions contributed to improved spatial understanding. Instructors observed more effective learning and higher performance on practical exams.

Challenges: Integrating AR technology into existing curricula required significant curriculum redesign and faculty training. Ensuring all students had access to AR-capable devices was also a concern.

Case Study 3: Language Learning with AR

Background: An elementary school introduced an AR language learning program to support English as a Second Language (ESL) students by providing interactive, contextual learning experiences.

Implementation: The program used AR flashcards and storytelling. Students could scan cards with a tablet to see animated characters and scenes related to the vocabulary words. Narratives and dialogues reinforced language skills in a meaningful context.

Outcomes: ESL students showed improved vocabulary retention and pronunciation skills. The interactive, visual nature of the AR content helped bridge language barriers, making learning more engaging and accessible for students with diverse language backgrounds.

Challenges: The main challenge was ensuring the technology was used to complement, not replace, traditional language learning strategies, requiring careful lesson planning and teacher facilitation.

These case studies underscore the transformative potential of VR and AR in education, from enhancing engagement and understanding in complex subjects to providing accessible and immersive Learning experiences.

While challenges such as cost, integration, and training persist, the positive outcomes highlight the value of investing in these technologies. As VR and AR continue to evolve, their role in education is set to expand, offering exciting possibilities for future teaching and learning innovations.

The role of educators in facilitating VR and AR learning experiences.

The role of educators in facilitating Virtual Reality (VR) and Augmented Reality (AR) learning experiences is pivotal to successfully integrating these technologies into educational settings.

As VR and AR redefine the boundaries of traditional learning, teachers are not just content deliverers but become guides, facilitators, and co-learners in a dynamic educational landscape. This discussion will explore educators' multifaceted roles in leveraging VR and AR to enhance learning outcomes.

Navigators of Technological Integration

Educators must navigate integrating VR and AR technologies into the curriculum, ensuring that their use aligns with educational goals and learning objectives. This involves:

- **Curriculum Integration**: Identifying opportunities within the curriculum where VR and AR can enhance understanding, engagement, and knowledge retention.
- **Technology Advocacy**: Championing the adoption of VR and AR technologies within educational institutions, highlighting their benefits to stakeholders.

Facilitators of Immersive Learning

In VR and AR environments, educators facilitate immersive learning experiences, guiding students through virtual simulations, explorations, and interactive scenarios. This role encompasses:

- **Guided Exploration**: I lead students through VR and AR experiences, prompting inquiry and encouraging critical thinking and reflection.
- **Adaptive Learning Support**: Adjusting learning experiences based on students' needs and responses within the VR or AR environment.

Designers of Interactive Content

Educators often contribute to designing and selecting VR and AR content, tailoring experiences to meet the specific needs of their students and subject matter. This creative role involves:

- **Content Customization**: Working with developers or using authoring tools to create or customise VR and AR experiences that align with lesson objectives.
- **Resource Curation**: Select high-quality VR and AR resources from available content libraries that effectively convey the intended learning outcomes.

Assessors of Learning Outcomes

The immersive nature of VR and AR offers new avenues for assessing student understanding and skills. Educators must develop and implement assessment strategies that accurately reflect learning within these environments, including:

- **Performance-Based Assessment**: Evaluating students' skills and knowledge based on their actions and decisions in virtual scenarios.

- **Reflective Debriefing**: Facilitating post-experience discussions to assess understanding, encourage reflection, and integrate learning with traditional curricular content.

Advocates for Equity and Accessibility

Educators play a crucial role in ensuring that VR and AR technologies are accessible to all students, advocating for resources and support to overcome barriers to access. This includes:

- **Equitable Access**: Striving to provide all students with access to VR and AR experiences, regardless of socio-economic status or disabilities.
- **Inclusive Design**: Promoting the development and selection of VR and AR content that is inclusive and representative of diverse student populations.

Lifelong Learners and Collaborators

The rapid evolution of VR and AR technologies necessitates that educators are lifelong learners, continuously updating their knowledge and skills. Collaboration with peers, technologists, and educational researchers is vital to share best practices, overcome challenges, and innovate using VR and AR in education.

- **Professional Development**: Participating in workshops, courses, and professional learning communities focused on VR and AR in education.
- **Interdisciplinary Collaboration**: Working with technology, pedagogy, and subject matter experts to create enriching and effective VR and AR learning experiences.

The successful implementation of VR and AR in education hinges on educators embracing new roles as facilitators, designers, assessors, and advocates. By navigating these roles effectively, teachers can unlock the full potential of immersive technologies to create engaging, personalised, and transformative learning experiences for their students.

As VR and AR continue to evolve, so will educators' dynamic role, shaping the future of educational technology and its impact on learning.

Examine the potential barriers to the widespread adoption of VR and AR in education.

Integrating Virtual Reality (VR) and Augmented Reality (AR) into educational settings holds immense potential for transforming teaching and learning processes. However, several barriers hinder their widespread adoption. By examining these challenges in detail, educators, policymakers, and technologists can strategise effective solutions to leverage the full potential of VR and AR in education.

Technical and Infrastructure Challenges

High Costs

The initial setup for VR and AR technologies, including hardware like headsets, compatible devices, and software licenses, can be relatively inexpensive for many educational institutions. This cost barrier limits accessibility, especially in underfunded schools.

Hardware and Software Compatibility

The diversity in VR and AR platforms and rapid technological advancements can lead to compatibility issues. Ensuring all students have access to compatible devices and keeping software up to date are ongoing challenges.

Infrastructure Requirements

Effective implementation of VR and AR requires robust digital infrastructure, including high-speed internet and digital learning environments. Schools in regions with limited technological infrastructure may need help to support these technologies.

Pedagogical Challenges

Integration into Curriculum

Integrating VR and AR into existing curricula requires thoughtful planning, development of new teaching materials, and alignment with educational standards and objectives. Educators must also be trained to seamlessly incorporate these technologies into their teaching strategies.

Assessment and Evaluation

Traditional assessment methods may not be suitable for the interactive and experiential learning experiences offered by VR and AR. Developing new strategies to assess student learning and progress in these environments can be challenging.

Teacher Training and Support

Teachers play a crucial role in successfully integrating VR and AR into education. However, many educators may need to become more familiar with these technologies or how to use them effectively. Providing adequate professional development and ongoing support is essential.

Ethical and Accessibility Challenges

Privacy and Data Security

VR and AR applications often collect and process personal data to create personalised learning experiences. Ensuring the privacy and security of this data is a significant concern, requiring strict adherence to data protection laws and ethical standards.

Equity and Access

There is a risk that the benefits of VR and AR could exacerbate educational inequalities if only students have access to these technologies. Ensuring equitable access for all students, including those from disadvantaged backgrounds or with disabilities, is a critical challenge.

Content Appropriateness and Quality

Another barrier is developing high-quality, educationally appropriate VR and AR content that is diverse, inclusive, and free from biases. Content must be carefully curated and designed to meet the diverse needs of learners.

Social and Psychological Challenges

User Experience and Comfort

VR and AR experiences can vary significantly in quality and user-friendliness. Poorly designed applications may lead to discomfort, disorientation, or motion sickness, affecting the learning experience.

Technology Dependence and Isolation

There are concerns about the potential for technology dependence and the impact of immersive technologies on social skills and real-world interactions. Balancing VR and AR with traditional, interactive learning experiences is essential.

Overcoming the barriers to the widespread adoption of VR and AR in education requires a multifaceted approach involving investments in technology and infrastructure, professional development for educators, curriculum integration, development of assessment methods, and addressing ethical and accessibility concerns.

Collaborative efforts among educators, policymakers, technology providers, and communities are crucial to harnessing VR and AR's transformative potential in enriching educational experiences for all learners.

Investigating strategies for overcoming barriers

Investigating strategies for overcoming the barriers to the widespread adoption of Virtual Reality (VR) and Augmented Reality (AR) in education involves a comprehensive approach, addressing the technical, pedagogical, ethical, and accessibility challenges. By implementing these strategies, educational institutions can harness the potential of VR and AR technologies to enhance learning experiences.

Here are several key strategies:

Addressing Technical and Infrastructure Challenges

Leveraging Economies of Scale

Pooling resources within or across educational institutions can lower costs. Bulk purchasing agreements for hardware and software, shared VR/AR labs, and collaborative content development can make these technologies more affordable.

Ensuring Compatibility and Scalability

Selecting hardware and software solutions compatible with a wide range of devices and scalable to different class sizes and educational needs can minimise obsolescence and maximise reach.

Strengthening Digital Infrastructure

Investments in digital infrastructure, including high-speed internet access and digital learning platforms, are essential. Partnerships with technology companies and government initiatives can support infrastructure development in underserved areas.

Overcoming Pedagogical Challenges

Curriculum Integration Support

Developing guidelines and resources for integrating VR and AR into curricula can help educators effectively incorporate these technologies. Collaboration with curriculum developers and educational researchers is critical.

Innovative Assessment Methods

Creating new assessment tools and methods that align with the interactive and immersive nature of VR and AR can better evaluate student learning and engagement in these environments.

Professional Development Programs

Offering professional development programs focused on VR and AR can equip educators with the skills and confidence to use these technologies effectively. These programs should be ongoing to keep pace with technological advancements.

Tackling Ethical and Accessibility Challenges

Implementing Robust Privacy Protections

Adopting strict data protection measures and transparent privacy policies ensures the ethical use of VR and AR technologies. Educators and developers must know and comply with relevant data protection laws.

Promoting Equitable Access

Strategies to ensure equitable access include providing VR/AR equipment to schools in underserved communities, developing low-cost solutions, and ensuring that content is accessible to students with disabilities.

High-Quality, Inclusive Content Development

Developing high-quality, educationally relevant, and inclusive VR and AR content is crucial. This involves diverse teams in content creation and rigorous testing with diverse user groups.

Addressing Social and Psychological Challenges

Balancing Technology Use

Incorporating VR and AR as a balanced educational approach that includes traditional, interactive, and outdoor learning experiences can mitigate technology dependence and isolation concerns.

User Comfort and Safety

Designing VR and AR experiences prioritising user comfort and safety, including ergonomic designs and settings to limit session lengths, can improve the learning experience and reduce the risk of discomfort or motion sickness.

Overcoming the barriers to VR and AR adoption in education requires a collaborative and multifaceted approach involving educators, policymakers, technology providers, and the wider community.

By addressing technical, pedagogical, ethical, and accessibility challenges, the educational sector can unlock these technologies' transformative potential and create immersive, engaging, and inclusive learning experiences for all students.

Explore strategies for funding VR and AR initiatives in schools.

Funding Virtual Reality (VR) and Augmented Reality (AR) initiatives in schools is critical to integrating these innovative technologies into educational settings. Given the cost implications of VR and AR equipment, software, and content development, identifying effective funding strategies is essential for schools aiming to harness the potential of these tools for enhancing teaching and learning. Here are several strategies for securing funding for VR and AR initiatives in educational institutions:

1. Grants and Philanthropic Funding

Educational Grants

Many government agencies, educational foundations, and non-profit organisations offer grants to support technology integration in education. Schools can apply for grants targeting STEM (Science, Technology, Engineering, and Mathematics) education, innovation, or digital learning enhancements, often covering VR and AR projects.

Corporate Sponsorship

Technology companies and local businesses may be interested in sponsoring VR and AR initiatives as part of their corporate social responsibility (CSR) programs. Partnerships with these entities can provide funding and access to technology, expertise, and professional development resources.

2. Crowdfunding and Community Support

Crowdfunding Campaigns

Platforms like Kickstarter, GoFundMe, or DonorsChoose enable schools to reach out to the broader community for financial support. By creating compelling campaigns highlighting the educational benefits of VR and AR, schools can attract donations from individuals and organisations interested in supporting innovative educational tools.

Parent-Teacher Associations (PTAs)

Engaging PTAs and school boards can help garner support for VR and AR initiatives. These groups can organise fundraising events, drives, and community outreach efforts to raise funds and awareness about the benefits of integrating these technologies into the curriculum.

3. Partnerships and Collaborations

Educational Consortiums and Networks

Joining forces with other schools and educational institutions to form consortiums or networks can enable bulk purchasing of VR and AR equipment and content, resulting in significant cost savings. These partnerships can also facilitate shared access to resources and professional development opportunities.

Academic-Industry Partnerships

Collaborating with technology companies and industry partners can provide schools access to cutting-edge VR and AR technologies. These partnerships may include in-kind donations, access to proprietary software, and collaboration on curriculum development tailored to the technology.

4. Government and Educational Policy Support

State and Federal Funding Programs

Keeping abreast of state and federal education funding opportunities is crucial. Many governments fund digital learning technologies and infrastructure improvements, including VR and AR projects.

Policy Advocacy

Advocating for policies supporting technology integration in education can lead to increased funding opportunities. Engaging with policymakers, participating in educational forums, and contributing to policy discussions can help highlight the need for investment in VR and AR technologies.

5. Innovative Financing Models

Leasing or Subscription Services

Instead of purchasing VR and AR equipment outright, schools can consider leasing hardware or subscribing to software and content services. This can spread the cost over time and ensure access to the latest technology without significant upfront investments.

Internal Funding Reallocation

Schools can evaluate their current budgets and spending to identify areas where funds can be reallocated to support VR and AR initiatives. This might include redirecting funds from outdated technologies or underutilised resources.

Securing funding for VR and AR school initiatives requires a multifaceted approach, combining grants, community support, partnerships, policy engagement, and innovative financing models. By exploring these strategies, educational institutions can overcome financial barriers and leverage VR and AR technologies to enrich students' learning experiences.

Blockchain for Secure Educational Records

Initially devised for digital currencies like Bitcoin, blockchain technology has emerged as a promising solution for enhancing security, transparency, and verification in various sectors, including education. In the context of educational records, blockchain offers a decentralised and immutable ledger that can revolutionise how academic credentials are issued, stored, and shared.

This book explores the application of blockchain technology for securing educational records, highlighting its benefits, challenges, and potential implications for the future of academic credentialing.

Benefits of Using Blockchain for Educational Records

Enhanced Security and Integrity

Blockchain's decentralised nature means that records are not stored in a single location but are distributed across a network, making it extremely difficult for hackers to compromise the data. Additionally, once information enters the blockchain, it becomes immutable, preventing unauthorised alterations.

Streamlined Verification Process

The traditional process of verifying academic credentials is often time-consuming and prone to errors. Blockchain can simplify this process by providing a transparent and easily accessible ledger where educational records are permanently and securely stored. Institutions and employers can instantly verify the authenticity of academic credentials without contacting the issuing institution.

Reduced Costs and Administrative Burdens

Blockchain technology can automate the issuance and verification of educational records, significantly reducing the administrative workload on academic institutions and the associated costs. This automation also minimises the risk of human error in record keeping.

Improved Accessibility and Portability

Blockchain enables students to have lifelong, portable access to their academic records, regardless of where they earned their credits or degrees. This is particularly beneficial in today's globalised world, where individuals often move across borders for education and employment.

Challenges and Considerations

Technological Complexity and Implementation Costs

Implementing blockchain technology requires significant technical expertise and infrastructure, which can be costly. Educational institutions, especially those with limited resources, may need help with these initial hurdles.

Privacy Concerns

While blockchain can enhance the security of educational records, it also raises privacy concerns. Blockchain's transparency and immutability mean that once information is recorded, it cannot be altered or deleted, which might conflict with privacy laws and individuals' forgotten rights.

Standardisation and Interoperability

For blockchain to effectively manage educational records across different institutions and countries, there needs to be standardisation in how data is recorded and shared. Ensuring interoperability among various blockchain systems is crucial for seamless access and verification of records.

Legal and Regulatory Challenges

The legal framework surrounding the use of blockchain for educational records is still evolving. Institutions must navigate these legal considerations when implementing blockchain solutions, including data protection laws and accreditation requirements.

Future Implications

Adopting blockchain for educational records could lead to a more open, efficient, and global education system. It offers the potential for creating a universal credentialing and skill verification system, which could transform hiring practices and lifelong learning pathways.

As blockchain technology matures and these challenges are addressed, its integration into the education sector will likely accelerate, paving the way for a new era of secure, transparent, and accessible educational credentialing.

Blockchain Technology in Education

Blockchain technology presents a transformative solution for securing educational records, offering enhanced security, streamlined verification processes, and improved accessibility. However, its successful implementation requires overcoming significant technological complexity, privacy concerns, standardisation issues, and regulatory hurdles. As the education sector continues exploring and adopting blockchain, it is poised to revolutionise how educational achievements are recorded, shared, and verified in a digital age.

Investigating real-world examples of blockchain technology in education provides insight into how this innovative approach is being applied to secure and streamline the management of educational records. These examples highlight the practical benefits and challenges of integrating blockchain into educational systems and offer a glimpse into the future possibilities of credentialing and record-keeping in academia.

1. MIT's Digital Diploma Project

The Massachusetts Institute of Technology (MIT) launched a pilot project in 2017, issuing digital diplomas to graduates through an app called Blockcerts Wallet. This initiative allows students to securely own, share, and verify the authenticity of their diplomas with employers and institutions directly, without intermediaries. The blockchain-based system ensures that each digital diploma is tamper-proof and verifiable anywhere in the world.

2. Sony Global Education's Blockchain for Education

In partnership with IBM, Sony Global Education developed a blockchain-based system to centralise and secure student records from multiple educational institutions. This platform enables students to share their academic achievements and extracurricular activities seamlessly with schools and third parties, facilitating the application and recruitment processes. It also aims to enhance educational continuity for students moving between schools or countries.

3. The University of Nicosia's Use of Blockchain

The University of Nicosia (UNIC) in Cyprus is recognised as the first university in the world to accept Bitcoin for tuition payment and to offer a Master of Science degree in Digital Currency. Beyond these initiatives, UNIC uses blockchain to issue and verify academic certificates, positioning itself as a leader in applying blockchain technology in higher education. This approach has enhanced the transparency and international recognition of UNIC's credentials.

4. OpenCerts Platform in Singapore

Launched by the Singapore Ministry of Education and GovTech, the OpenCerts platform leverages blockchain technology to issue and validate tamper-resistant digital academic certificates for students in Singapore. This initiative streamlines the certificate verification process for employers and educational institutions, reducing the administrative burden and enhancing the integrity of academic records.

5. The APPII Platform

APPII, an intelligent careers platform, utilises blockchain technology to verify its users' CVs. This includes academic achievements, professional qualifications, and membership in professional bodies. By ensuring the authenticity of educational and professional credentials, APPII simplifies the hiring process for employers and helps individuals stand out with verified CV information.

Challenges and Insights

These real-world applications of blockchain in education illustrate the technology's potential to revolutionise how academic credentials are issued, stored, and shared. However, they also highlight challenges such as the need for widespread adoption, interoperability between different blockchain systems, and ongoing privacy concerns. Despite these hurdles, the successful implementation of blockchain for educational records in these examples points to a future where academic credentials are more secure, verifiable, and accessible.

The Technical Foundation of Blockchain and its Application

Blockchain technology's application in securing educational records is proving to be a viable and innovative solution to many of the challenges facing the management of academic credentials today. As more institutions explore and adopt blockchain, it will likely become a standard practice in education, offering a more transparent, efficient, and secure way to manage and verify educational achievements.

Exploring the technical foundation of blockchain technology and its application across various sectors provides a comprehensive understanding of its capabilities, limitations, and potential for transformation. Blockchain's core principles of decentralisation, transparency, and immutability underpin its diverse applications, extending far beyond its initial use in digital currencies to fields such as education, healthcare, supply chain management, and more.

Technical Foundation of Blockchain

Decentralisation

Unlike traditional databases managed by a central authority, blockchain technology distributes its data across a network of computers (nodes). This decentralisation ensures that no single point of failure can compromise the system's integrity, enhancing security and resilience.

Transparency and Trust

Blockchain technology operates on a consensus mechanism, where multiple nodes must verify all transactions based on predefined rules before being added to the ledger. This process ensures transparency and builds trust among participants without the need for intermediaries.

Immutability

Once a transaction is recorded on a blockchain, it cannot be altered or deleted. This immutability is ensured through cryptographic hash functions, which generate a unique digital fingerprint for each block. Any attempt to tamper with the transaction data would be immediately evident and rejected by the network.

Additional resources for educators interested in blockchain technology.

A wealth of resources is available for educators interested in integrating blockchain technology into their curriculum or understanding its impact on the education sector. These resources range from academic courses and professional development workshops to online platforms and scholarly articles, all designed to provide educators with the knowledge and tools needed to navigate the burgeoning field of blockchain in education. Below is a review of various resources that can enrich educators' proficiency in blockchain technology.

Online Courses and Certifications

1. **Blockchain Specializations on Coursera and edX**: Platforms like Coursera and edX offer comprehensive courses in blockchain technology, covering its principles, applications, and implications. Leading universities often develop courses and include topics tailored for educators looking to incorporate blockchain into their teaching.

2. **Udemy Blockchain Courses**: Udemy features a range of courses on blockchain technology, from introductory to advanced levels. These courses can help educators understand the technical aspects of blockchain and explore its educational applications.

3. **Blockchain Council**: Offers certifications for various blockchain-related roles, providing deep dives into blockchain technology and its use cases. Such certifications can be valuable for educators seeking to specialise in this area.

Professional Development Workshops and Seminars

1. **Educational Technology Conferences**: ISTE (International Society for Technology in Education) and SXSW EDU often feature workshops and seminars on the latest technology trends, including blockchain. These events provide opportunities for educators to learn from experts and network with peers interested in blockchain.

2. **Blockchain in Education Workshops**: Some organisations and educational institutions offer workshops for teachers and administrators. These workshops focus on implementing blockchain for secure records, credentialing, and enhancing the learning experience.

Scholarly Articles and Journals

1. **Journal of Blockchain Education & Research**: This peer-reviewed journal publishes research and insights on integrating blockchain technology in education, offering case studies, theoretical analyses, and reviews of current practices.

2. **Educause Review**: A reputable source for higher education IT and technology integration articles, including insightful pieces on blockchain's potential and challenges in educational settings.

Online Platforms and Communities

1. **LinkedIn Groups and Professional Networks**: Joining blockchain-focused groups on platforms like LinkedIn can facilitate connections with blockchain experts and educators. These communities often share resources, discuss challenges, and provide support for integrating blockchain into educational contexts.

2. **Reddit and Online Forums**: Platforms such as Reddit have active communities dedicated to blockchain technology, where educators can ask questions, share experiences, and find resources curated by blockchain enthusiasts and professionals.

Books and Educational Guides

1. **"Blockchain Revolution" by Don and Alex Tapscott**: This book provides a comprehensive overview of blockchain technology and its potential impact across various sectors, including education.

2. **"Blockchain for Education: A Research Companion"** is a compilation of research and case studies examining the use of blockchain in educational settings, offering

insights into its practical applications and future directions.

As blockchain technology continues to evolve and new applications in education are found, it is crucial for educators to stay informed and educated on this topic.

By leveraging the above resources, educators can better understand blockchain technology, explore its educational applications, and contribute to shaping the future of secure, transparent, and innovative learning environments.

Predictive Analytics in Student Success

Predictive analysis in education is a type of analytic concerning educational data that predicts prospective student trends and outcomes with behaviour. The collection and analysis of information include grades, class attendance records, interaction in learning platforms, and social-emotional factors. This means that educators can even identify patterns and insights that may not be obvious through machine learning algorithms and statistical models.

On the other end, predictive analytics in education cover quite an enormous scope. This entails predicting the learner's future performances, identifying those at risk of failing, and recommending the most appropriate interventions to help.

This technology may also assist in customising learning paths according to the student's pace, interests, and needs. On the other hand, predictive analytics will ensure that resources are deployed most effectively and efficiently, focusing on efforts and investments where most need to be done by academic institutions.

They provide insights to educators and administrators on establishing an empowering environment for each student to succeed by using the power within the data.

Predictive analytics represent a broad spectrum of benefits that enhance student success. Therefore, education becomes more responsible and adjustable to individual needs. The principal added value comes from personalised learning experiences. Such educators engage in personalised learning, meaning that they draw from student interactions and performance data to mould their learning material and approaches according to the needs and styles of individual students.

This helps narrow the learning gap and build upon strengths rather than fix problems, which should improve student engagement and outcomes.
Another critical benefit is the early identification of at-risk students. Predictive models can flag students who may need additional support long before they fail a course or drop out. This early warning system enables timely interventions, such as tutoring, counselling, or adjustments in course load, significantly increasing the chances of student retention and success.

Moreover, predictive analytics enhances **decision-making for educators and administrators**. Insights derived from data analysis can inform curriculum development, resource allocation, and policy formulation, ensuring that educational strategies are evidence-based and focused on improving student outcomes.

In essence, predictive analytics transforms education into a more data-driven and outcome-oriented endeavour, ultimately fostering an environment where every student has the opportunity to thrive.

Several educational institutions have successfully implemented predictive analytics to improve student success. For instance, **Georgia State University** used predictive analytics to identify and support at-risk students, significantly improving graduation rates. Analysing historical data, the university developed an early alert system that notifies advisors when a student appears off track. This proactive approach resulted in reduced dropout rates and increased graduation.

Another example is **Purdue University**, which developed a "Course Signals" system to predict students' performance. The system can forecast their grades early in the semester by leveraging student engagement, effort, and academic performance data. This allows for timely interventions, such as personalised feedback and additional resources, helping students improve their performance before it's too late.

These case studies highlight the practical benefits of predictive analytics in enhancing student success. By identifying at-risk students early and providing personalised interventions, educational institutions can significantly improve outcomes, demonstrating the powerful impact of data-driven strategies in education.

While predictive analytics holds great promise for enhancing student success, it also poses challenges and ethical considerations. **Data privacy** is a primary concern, as collecting and analysing student data requires stringent measures to protect sensitive information. Institutions must balance leveraging data for student benefit and respecting individual privacy rights.

Using student data is a big ethical question, depending on how fair or unbiased interventions apply predictive analytics. In some cases, algorithms could perpetuate biases already in effect and negatively affect some student groups. Continuous oversight and adjustment should maintain fairness and inclusivity.

It would, therefore, require clear policies, ethical guidelines, and dedication to the good of students so that they feel empowered and not discriminated against in using this predictive tool. The future of predictive analytics within the education domain is expected to be very positive due to the advancement of technologies and machine learning, which provides relatively new opportunities for further enhancing student success.

Leading trends like adaptive learning technologies and AI-driven tutoring systems are poised to make education more personal and meet ever-changing needs for diverse learning methods. The kind of technology likely to develop is creating power in much finer, more nuanced educational interventions through predictive analytics.

Therefore, the key to making good on these advances lies in ethical use combined with an unyielding focus on fair outcomes and continuous improvement that allows predictive analytics to remain a powerfully positive change in education.

Predictive analysis in the education sector will be the new frontier that opens with data-driven decision-making, opening up opportunities to serve and enhance student success in previously impossible ways. Educators and institutions can use this predictive analytic ability to customise learning experiences, identify at-risk students significantly earlier, and hasten educational strategies to serve students' different needs.

Despite the challenges and ethical concerns, the benefits approached mindfully make it look like an overwhelmingly positive case. With the development of technology, predictive analytic capabilities will also develop, making education more flexible, responsive, and efficient in meeting the needs of every student. Embracing this future requires commitment, innovation, and a steadfast focus on student well-being and success.

CHAPTER 7

Exploring the Horizon: Role of AI in Enhancing Language Teaching and Learning Methodologies.

The infusion of Artificial Intelligence (AI) in language education is revolutionary and transformative, having the potential to change a lot more than the very methodology of teaching: indeed, "the basic framework" of language acquisition processes. Technology integration has delivered inventive methods that make language learning even more accessible, efficient, and enjoyable than ever.

Also, integrating technology has brought inventive methods that facilitate individual learning preferences.

The book, therefore, discusses the nuanced use of AI in the domain of language teaching and learning: delves into areas like personalised learning, improvement of communication skills, the role AI plays in cultural immersion with its difficulties, and probably a practical future course that it is bound to chart out on an educational landscape.

Personalised Learning: Tailoring Education to Individual Needs

He discusses offering individualised education and states that AI has already positioned itself as central to learning languages.

Traditional language teaching methods sometimes fail to solve the learners' diverse needs, and disparities arise.

This is a function that AI performs in adaptive learning technologies. It analyses how learners interact with questions and their corresponding performances in line with the content, pace, and learning paths, giving them a personalised adjustment.

This would involve exercise recommendations on improving the identified weaknesses in vocabulary, grammar, or pronunciation, thus optimising the process for efficiency and effectiveness.

Enhancing Communication Skills: **Beyond Grammar and Vocabulary**

Accuracy, vocabulary, and grammar are building blocks for language, but mastering these skills is necessary for effective communication. On the other hand, tools like speech recognition work with AI through Natural Language Processing (NLP) to facilitate the required learning.

There are tools for such instant feedback of pronunciation, voice modulation, and fluency, enabling immediate correction and learning.

The conversational AI assistant offers interactive dialogue in the target language, whereby the user can practice conversation with real people around him, though in a controlled and not entirely natural environment.

Interaction is critical to help users increase their confidence and build the competence needed to use language in real life for teaching and learning languages, including Artificial Intelligence (AI), which has brought about technological advancement.

AI has introduced tools that progress the tedious method of teaching and learning a language towards a more interactive, individualised, and efficient process.

Below are essential AI tools in language education, giving an example to illustrate the impact and application.

1. Adaptive Learning Platforms Example: Duolingo

AI algorithms support adaptive learning platforms that personalise learning toward individual performance and preferences. Duolingo, one of the most downloaded apps for language learning, applies AI to adjust the lessons to the learner's strengths and weaknesses.

This algorithm evaluates the user's answer to produce future exercises that best fit the learner's abilities without boring him with too-easy material or overwhelming him with too-tricky content.

This personalises and enhances the learning process as the student works on areas that need improvement.

2. Natural Language Processing (NLP) for Language Assessment

Example: Write & Improve

NLP technologies read and respond to language use, specifically in writing. "Write & Improve" is a newly developed AI technology tool for instant, on-the-go writing assessment and feedback; it is at "Write & Improve" by Cambridge English researchers.

They submit uploaded written work, which this tool will analyse and suggest improving grammar, vocabulary, and spelling. In this case, instant feedback increases the learning speed since learners can immediately see areas in which they are weak and learn how to improve these areas.

3. Speech Recognition for Pronunciation Training

Example: ELSA Speak

Students can use new speech recognition technology to analyse and improve their pronunciation. For a long time, this has been the limiting factor when practising another language in the traditional classroom.

A handy app for learning pronunciation is the ELSA Speak AI English Pronunciation app, which listens to what users speak and proceeds by giving feedback on the precision in pronouncing, fluency pitch, intonation, etc.

It uses cutting-edge speech recognition technology to pinpoint precisely which sounds were not pronounced right and offers exercises to practise that particular sound. This kind of technology would make it easier and more feasible for the student to be proficient in the sound of any foreign language.

4. Chatbots for Conversational Practice

Example: Mondly

Conversational AI chatbots offer learners an ideal opportunity to practice language in a conversational way that significantly affects fluency and confidence. Mondly is an application in language learning apps that uses an AI-powered chatbot to conduct learners in simulated conversations.

These interactions replicate human conversational dynamics, offering a safe and engaging environment for practising the learner's spoken and listening skills. The AI chatbot responds dynamically to the learner's inputs, making the conversation suitable for both the learner's level and progress.

5. Virtual Reality (VR) for Immersive Learning

Example: ImmerseMe

These include platforms such as ImmerseMe, on which learners could have language practice in virtual environments. For example, AI-powered VR technology allows students to learn languages by immersing themselves in lifelike experiences. ImmerseMe is a platform that gives students an opportunity.

From ordering food in a French café to asking for directions in Tokyo, ImmerseMe puts the learners in the usual real-life situations where they can apply the language.

This type of learning attaches language use to experience; hence, learners find it easy to get concepts and remember everything they are learning.

6. Machine Translation for Language Learning

Example: Google Translate

Although not a learning tool by itself, tools such as Google Translate support learning because the learners can consult the translation of words, expressions, or texts at once. Nevertheless, judiciously applied, they may greatly help vocabulary acquisition and comprehension.

At the same time, the presence of a pronunciation guide and the ability to listen to the translated text help develop the learner's pronunciation and listening skills.

Challenges and Future Directions

Nevertheless, for all the positives, AI tools in language learning come with their challenges: issues of overreliance on technology, possible inaccuracies, and an impersonal character in some AI interactions may remind us how important the human factor is in education.

Thus, the future of language learning is somehow related to the involvement of AI in parallel with human teachers, where all the peculiarities of language will be taught using AI's strengths and human irreproducible qualities.

Development and improvement of AI-based language teaching and learning tools will further progress, with innovations constantly arising. As these tools continue to develop, promising increased accessibility, personalisation, and practicality for using them to help learn languages, they will further revolutionise language education. Cultural Immersion: Bridging Languages with Cultures

Learning a language comes with cultural understanding. AI with VR (virtual reality) and AR (augmented reality) are opening up new vistas of cultural immersion, enabling the learner to partake in the language one is learning right from their artistic background.

Powered by AI, the immersive simulation allows students to take virtual trips to foreign locales and interact with AI-driven characters to experience learning from related scenarios. In this manner, it amplifies language skills and culturally deepens an empathic feeling, thus giving a holistic learning of language.

Automated Assessment: **Shaping the Future of Language Evaluation**

The role of AI continues in the assessment sector, with tools that allow far more objectivity and consistency in measuring language proficiency. These tools include automated essay scoring and spoken language assessment, which uses NLP to analyse language use and provide in-depth feedback on many areas of language proficiency.

Indicating the ability to carry out more and fuller assessments guides the learner through a more informed and focused language learning journey.

Challenges and Ethical Considerations

Despite these advancements, integrating AI into language education is challenging.

Data privacy, algorithmic bias, and the digital divide pose significant ethical and logistical concerns. A couple of problems are also noticed: one is related to dependence on AI tools, and the other concerns the dilution of human interaction in the learning process of a language, which in turn can affect soft skills and those cultural nuances that AI can't replicate in entirety.

The Future of AI in Language Learning

AI will indeed bring more to teaching and learning language. As the applications of AI technologies increase with advancements in language education, more is bound to emerge.

Future developments may also see AI contributing to even more personalised and "in situ" learning experiences, making language learning feel more natural and intuitive, like the first language acquisition.

However, very reasonable navigation of AI-induced issues will be required so that technological advances ideally contribute to, rather than detract from, the human elements critical to successful language learning.

The integration of Artificial Intelligence in language learning and teaching opens windows to new horizons. Consequently, AI has added massive value to the language learning landscape by personalising the learning experience, strengthening communication skills, experiencing culture, and improving assessment.

Therefore, the way forward is to balance the scale so that it maximises AI's strengths and attends to its weaknesses and ethical issues.

With this new beginning in education, AI will undoubtedly be part of defining the future of language teaching and learning toward a world increasingly surmounting the promise language barriers hold.

Whether in personalisation, engagement, or accessibility, AI in language learning is a promising opportunity to redefine traditional education paradigms without precedent.

In contrast, developing AI technologies are set to continue deepening their impact on language learning, poised to provide progressively immersive, intuitive, and efficient means of acquiring new languages.

This looking-forward horizon envisages a landscape where AI should, in fact, complement and, to some extent, substitute conventional educational methodologies with its scalability, adaptability, and potential personalisation by its use.

Enhanced Personalization through Deep Learning

Future AI systems will depend on deep learning algorithms to more precisely analyse learners' behaviours, preferences, and performance. This, therefore, will lead to highly personalised learning paths that are supposed to change "in real time" and offer individualised education to each learner.

For example, AI can predict some of the challenges a learner may face with specific language constructs and, hence, can foresee such situations to prepare the curriculum in advance.

The granularity of personalisation will move beyond pace and content to include motivational messages and feedback styles attuned to the learner and cultural content tuned to the learner's interests and learning goals.

Seamless Integration of Augmented and Virtual Reality

Thus, combining AR and VR with AI will produce interactive language learning settings that, to the smallest detail, will reproduce interactions and scenarios from real life at the authentic level reached for the first time.

Students will be encouraged to immerse themselves in the technology as they apply their language skills within required contexts and environments—from an active city square in Rome to a peaceful park in Kyoto.

Future AI may craft dynamic, interactive scenarios based on the learner's progress so that every virtual visit solidifies the learner's learning journey.

Conversational AI and Advanced Natural Language Processing For example, improvements in conversational AI and natural language processing (NLP) would also give these AI tutors much more sophisticated and natural conversations with the learners.

Such AI tutors will be knowledgeable and able to generate human-like responses, perhaps even intuitive enough to identify the subtleties of language use or, in some scenarios, interpret emotional signals from the learner's speech or textual inputs.

This feature would ensure the learners have an easily accessible partner for practice and that they get instant feedback and correction following the simulated conversation interactions with the partner, just like live tutoring from a human.

Bridging the Gap with Neural Machine Translation

These Neural Machine Translation (NMT) technologies will evolve over the years, making very context-sensitive translations possible. Such a development will help any language learner by offering reliable, on-time translations that consider even the slightest nuances in the context of speech and culture.

Further, integration of NMT with Language Learning Tools will offer a way to ensure the alternation of languages by the learners is smooth, promote comparative learning, and still allow the perception of language structures and lexical contexts much better for the learners.

Ethical AI and Accessibility This shall be the future of AI in language learning, which also considers ethics and accessibility. This ensures inclusivity and makes language learning tools available to the various needed learners, including people with disabilities.

Ethical AI practices, in turn, will prioritise data privacy and security mechanisms for bias mitigation, meaning that AI language learning tools are built to be trustworthy and fair.

Challenges and Considerations The path to fully realising such promise with AI in language learning has its share of difficulties. These include the critical importance of equal access to technology, the right balance between technology and human interface, and the colossal digital divide.

In the future, AI in language learning will be seen as an "all hands on deck" approach involving educators, technologists, and policymakers working together to leverage AI's gains while grappling with its challenges.

The future of AI in language learning is supposed to revolutionise how languages are taught and learned, moving toward ever more personalised, engaging, and accessible education in languages.

The burgeoning of AI technologies will bring more opportunities and improvements to new language learners who practise and learn different languages and cultures. It will help reduce the communication barrier and promote a better global understanding.

Therefore, if attention is paid to AI's potential, the future of language learning could be far more inclusive, effective, and even more prosperous for learners worldwide.

Case Studies: AI Applications in Education

Duolingo - Revolutionizing Language Learning Through AI

Duolingo, an acclaimed language education leader, has revolutionised how we learn languages by integrating artificial intelligence to create a tailored educational journey for each user. This application of AI demonstrates the power of technology to make learning languages not just more accessible and efficient but also thoroughly enjoyable.

Innovative AI Applications in Language Learning with Duolingo

- Tailored Educational Journeys: Duolingo uses AI to craft individualised learning experiences. Analysing users' performance fine-tunes the difficulty and type of exercises in real-time, optimising learning trajectories for maximum progress.

- Advancements in Speech Recognition: Incorporating state-of-the-art speech recognition, Duolingo allows users to perfect their pronunciation. This immediate feedback mechanism encourages learners to refine their spoken language abilities swiftly.

- Learning Through Play: The platform employs AI to make learning a game, with points, levels, and rewards to engage users. It keeps track of user participation and adjusts challenges to keep the learning process captivating.

Duolingo's Reach and Accessibility

- A Universal Platform: Duolingo serves a broad audience, providing over 30 language courses to learners at all levels. Its intuitive interface welcomes users of every age group.

- Commitment to Inclusivity: With a design that prioritises accessibility, Duolingo features support for users with disabilities, ensuring everyone has the opportunity to learn.

Transformative Impact on Language Education

- Making Learning Accessible: Duolingo has dismantled traditional barriers to language education, such as cost and availability, opening up new horizons for millions globally.

- Enhancing Retention: The personalised approach, powered by AI, has significantly improved retention rates, enabling learners to reach their language learning goals more effectively.

- Encouraging Global Connection: Duolingo nurtures global connectivity and cultural exchange, enriching the learning experience by offering a plethora of languages.

Duolingo's success underscores the transformative potential of AI in language learning, providing a glimpse into the future of educational technology.

Implementing Adaptive Learning in STEM Education

Integrating adaptive learning into STEM education represents a comprehensive and multi-layered strategy to revolutionise the educational landscape. This approach is grounded in the selection of pertinent subjects, the adoption and integration of cutting-edge adaptive technologies, and the meticulous training of educators to utilise these innovations adeptly. The ultimate objective is to enrich the educational experience, ensuring it is in harmony with the curriculum's aspirations and the desired learning outcomes.

Strategic Selection of STEM Subjects

1. **Identifying Key Subjects:** The journey begins with identifying fundamental STEM subjects poised to benefit immensely from adaptive learning technologies. Special consideration is given to disciplines where students encounter considerable challenges or a significant disparity in achievement levels exists.

2. **Curriculum Evaluation:** The current curriculum is exhaustively evaluated to pinpoint areas for implementing adaptive learning. This process involves identifying topics that students traditionally find challenging and recognising opportunities where personalised learning pathways could significantly boost comprehension and retention.

Development and Integration of Adaptive Technologies

1. **Choosing the Right Technologies:** The subsequent phase involves carefully selecting adaptive learning technologies, favouring those that leverage AI and machine learning algorithms to analyse student data and tailor instructional content dynamically and meticulously.

2. **Collaborative Content Creation:** Developing adaptive learning content for STEM subjects is a collaborative endeavour, necessitating the synergy of subject matter experts, instructional designers, and technology specialists. This collective effort results in interactive and engaging content that aligns with learning goals and is responsive to students' nuanced needs.

3. **Seamless Curriculum Integration:** Incorporating adaptive learning technologies into the extant STEM curriculum demands thoughtful planning. This ensures that these technological advancements augment rather than supplant traditional teaching methodologies with adaptive content meticulously aligned with established curriculum standards and learning outcomes.

Empowering Educators with Adaptive Tools

1. **Comprehensive Educator Training:** Educators are afforded extensive training on the intricacies of adaptive learning technologies. This instruction spans the technical aspects of the platforms and delves into strategies for seamlessly integrating adaptive tools into classroom pedagogy.

2. **Robust Support Systems:** Establishing robust support systems is crucial, bolstering educators' confidence in employing adaptive learning technologies. This support framework includes access to technical assistance, the cultivation of a community of practice, and the encouragement of exchanging experiences and best practices among educators.

3. **Iterative Feedback Mechanism:** The implementation blueprint encompasses mechanisms for the systematic collection of feedback from both students and educators regarding the efficacy of the adaptive learning tools. This feedback is a cornerstone for continuously refining adaptive learning content and strategies.

Successfully implementing adaptive learning in STEM education necessitates deliberate planning, collaborative effort, and unwavering support. By concentrating on these pivotal areas, educational institutions can forge dynamic and responsive learning environments that cater to the diverse needs of STEM learners, culminating in enhanced engagement and superior academic achievements.

Overview of TechForward Academy

TechForward Academy, at the forefront of STEM education, embraces a diverse student population, each with unique skills and learning preferences. Acknowledging the inherent challenges in delivering a fair and practical education to such a varied group, the academy has pioneered integrating adaptive learning technologies into its STEM curriculum. This initiative aims to personalise education, ensuring it meets the individual needs of each student.

Tailored Adaptive Technologies at TechForward Academy

1. ***AI-Enhanced Learning Management System (LMS):*** TechForward has incorporated an advanced LMS that uses artificial intelligence to create adaptive learning pathways. This system analyses students' performance data in real-time, customising content and assessments to suit each learner's needs.

2. ***Interactive STEM Simulations:*** The academy has introduced adaptive simulations for subjects like physics and chemistry, which vary in complexity based on each student's progress and comprehension. These simulations aim to deepen engagement and understanding of complex STEM concepts.

3. ***Dynamic Assessment Tools:*** Adaptive tools have been implemented to adjust the difficulty of questions in response to students' answers. This ensures that assessments are appropriately challenging, providing a true reflection of each student's knowledge and highlighting areas for improvement.

Navigating Implementation Challenges

1. Technical Integration: Merging new technologies with existing infrastructure presented notable hurdles. The solution involved forming a specialised IT integration team to ensure a smooth transition and compatibility between new and existing systems.

2. *Educator Onboarding:* Comprehensive training sessions overcame some educators' initial hesitation, as they feared adaptive technologies would replace traditional teaching methods. These sessions emphasised the complementary nature of adaptive technologies and were supported by ongoing assistance to alleviate concerns.

3. *Student Adaptation:* Introducing a more personalised learning environment was initially daunting for some students. To ease this transition, TechForward gradually introduced adaptive tools, complemented by workshops that showcased their benefits and practical use.

Outcomes and Reflections

- *Enhanced Academic Performance:* Following adopting adaptive learning technologies, TechForward markedly improved STEM subject test scores, especially in areas where students traditionally underperformed.

- *Increased Engagement:* Student engagement significantly increased, evidenced by increased time spent on learning platforms and active participation in interactive simulations.

- *Positive Feedback Loop:* Feedback from students and educators has been overwhelmingly positive, highlighting the benefits of personalised learning paths and immediate feedback as key to the enhanced STEM curriculum.

This case study of TechForward Academy showcases the transformative impact of adaptive learning technologies on STEM education. By catering to students' individual learning needs, fostering greater engagement with interactive content, and equipping educators with advanced instructional tools, adaptive learning is set to illuminate the path forward in education.

AI-powered Educational Games and Simulations

The infusion of Artificial Intelligence (AI) into educational games and simulations heralds a groundbreaking shift in the landscape of learning technologies. This integration significantly enriches academic content's interactive and immersive qualities, offering a tailored educational journey that adjusts to each learner's unique pace, style, and preferences. Through this personalisation, AI renders learning more productive and accessible, catering to diverse student diversities.

Revolutionising Learning through AI-Enhanced Educational Tools

AI technologies, encompassing machine learning algorithms and natural language processing, are at the forefront of transforming educational games and simulations into dynamic and responsive learning environments. These sophisticated tools can meticulously analyse student interactions, anticipate challenges, and fine-tune the difficulty level or recommend specific resources on the fly. This adaptive approach to learning ensures a balance that avoids overwhelming or under-stimulating the student, thus maintaining a consistently engaging and fruitful educational experience.

The Transformative Impact of AI-Enabled Learning Tools

The essence of AI-powered educational games and simulations lies in their capacity to seamlessly meld traditional educational methodologies with the preferences of the digital-native cohort.

These tools captivate learners by providing immersive experiences that conventional classroom settings might fail to deliver. Moreover, they unlock the potential for hands-on exploration of intricate concepts and systems, rendering abstract or formidable topics more graspable and relatable.

1. **Tailored Educational Experiences:** AI's prowess in customising learning materials to match individual learners' specific requirements and progression pace marks a significant milestone in educational technology. This customisation ensures learning is more efficient, impactful, and perfectly aligned with the learner's objectives.

2. **Elevating Engagement:** By embedding elements of gamification and interactive simulations, AI-enhanced tools elevate the learning experience to new heights of engagement and enjoyment. Such an enriched learning environment motivates learners, particularly in areas they might find less appealing or more challenging.

3. **Broadening Accessibility:** AI-powered educational platforms extend their benefits to diverse learning needs, including accommodations for students with disabilities. Innovations like voice recognition, text-to-speech capabilities, and adaptive user interfaces ensure that these educational tools are accessible to every learner.

4. **Immediate Feedback for Accelerated Learning:** Providing real-time feedback is critical to the learning process. AI-driven games and simulations offer instant evaluations of a student's performance, delivering

corrective insights and explanations that reinforce understanding and retention of the subject matter.

The emergence of AI within educational games and simulations signals a formidable advance in crafting more effective, engaging, and inclusive educational tools.

As these technologies continue to evolve, their influence on educational practices and outcomes is set to expand, opening new pathways for enhancing the academic journey and equipping learners for the challenges of a rapidly evolving global landscape.

CHAPTER 8

Training Programs for Teachers on AI Tools

In this dynamically fast-moving world of technologies, artificial intelligence (AI) is becoming a vast game-changer force in reimagining and changing diverse domains, and education is no different in this regard. As AI tools enter education, they unlock doors to tailored learning experiences streamlined administrative work, and foster dynamic, responsive educational spaces.

However, the essence of using AI in education will depend on how ready educators are to use AI skilfully. This discourse has shown a need for meticulously crafted training programs to equip educators with the requisite expertise to exploit AI's capabilities to foster educational excellence.

The Role of AI in Reimagining Education

Much more than a technology buzzword, AI is leading a fundamental change in educational methodologies, moving toward personalised and engaging learning journeys. AI is a technology that uses adaptive learning algorithms to customise and adjust all education content to the learner's need and speed of learning, hence ensuring the involvement and success of the learner.

Third, amongst the power of AI is the capability that allows the automation of dreary, routine, and time-consuming administrative tasks, freeing educators to expend their time more on pedagogical efforts and less on bureaucratic stuff. The educational field is just beginning to explore the potential of AI worldwide, from AI-based tools for instruction to grading mechanisms and even virtual teaching assistants, which would mean an entirely new step in educational practices.

Educators' Preparedness for AI: A Current Snapshot

That said, looking at the brightest possibilities for AI in education, one observes a noticeable gap in how prepared educators are to integrate AI smoothly into their pedagogical fabric. Incomplete training initiatives and resource accessibility constraints endemic to technological shifts exacerbate this resistance.

Research-based findings and survey evidence consistently point out the urgent need for specific professional development in this area because teachers worry about AI integration. This further exacerbates the disparities between the two educational settings regarding readiness and the uneven distribution of resources.

Essential Elements of AI Training Programs for Educators

Certain elements must be part of effective AI training programs for educators. These include building the principles and ethical considerations foundational to AI and providing educators with a precise understanding of what AI technologies can or cannot do.

Develop practical applications that directly engage AI tools relevant to educational settings so that the educator becomes capable and much more confident in applying these technologies.

This may also contribute to the ethos of an in-service training or ongoing professional development program, which is necessary to ensure that educators are updated with the latest AI developments and pedagogical methods.

Overcoming Hurdles in AI Training Program Implementation:

The barriers to deploying AI training initiatives for educators run the gamut—from resource allocation to the imperative to tailor programs to varying technological proficiencies. Financial and infrastructural limitations often hinder building and delivering a solid training program.

However, partnering with tech firms and using online platforms would suffice as an alternative to dealing with these challenges. Efforts to personalise training to the different levels of technological ability between educators assure full inclusion of all the participants and allow them to learn much more effectively.

A Glimpse into Successful AI Training Ventures

In case study narratives of successful AI training programs for educators, dive into the strategies and their impacts. Of evidence is a case study where AI literacy was included in the educators' professional development curriculum, which showed marked improvements in teacher confidence and student engagement.

This success highlights the effectiveness of an all-encompassing training approach, in which the trainees are imparted practical, hands-on skills to accompany their theoretical knowledge.

As AI tools start to make inroads into education, the promise of transformation in the dynamics of teaching and learning dawns on. This recognition of the transformative promise is based on a shared commitment to ensuring educators have the possibility and recognition of capacity and knowledge to embrace AI's possibilities.

This shall remain an essential cornerstone of formulating and conducting the prioritised comprehensive training programs, ensuring educators are well-equipped to spearhead the integration of AI in enriching learners' experiences worldwide.

Policy Frameworks for AI in Education

On a further path, as we head more and more into the AI-infused future merging unilaterally with the very grain of our daily existence, AI adoption into the sphere of education is poised at nothing less than revolutionary in the conventional dynamics of pedagogy and the learners' disposition.

The promise of AI to customise learning experiences, streamline administrative operations, and unveil deep insights into academic performances is simply unmatchable.

However, this brisk adoption of AI in education also prompts pivotal considerations concerning ethical usage, data privacy, and equal access. Therefore, the call for comprehensive policy frameworks guiding AI's moral and productive integration in education becomes even more pronounced within this background.

This paper addresses the need for such frameworks, outlines their essential elements, and dwells on the issues in their formulation while looking at global perspectives and case studies.

The Imperative for Policy Frameworks in AI-Driven Education

On the one hand, AI is laying siege to the educational domain, throwing up many opportunities to improve quality and learning results. However, such a broad embrace of AI is not without its perils and, therefore, demands articulation on how clear policy frameworks should be laid out.

Without such frameworks, fundamental questions arise about privacy because AI systems require a lot of personal data for optimal operation.

Along the same line, such latent biases in AI algorithms may further exaggerate or solidify existing educational disparities and fall, therefore, unfairly far against students who hail from underrepresented backgrounds. Similarly, uneven distribution of resources through AI may make room for a digital divide and thus derail equity principles in the education system.

These circumstances underscore the need for a policy framework to suggest the responsible, ethical, and inclusive deployment of AI within educational contexts.

Crucial Elements of Effective AI Policy Frameworks for Education

Ethical Considerations
However, all AI policy frameworks need to address ethical dilemmas. The policy imposes transparent data use, whereby all stakeholders must be assured of how student data is handled or protected. Strict measures regarding privacy issues include explicit data consent and stringent security protocols.

Periodic assessments of the bias these AI systems carry should also be checked. They are indispensable to ensuring this technology does not amplify existing education disparities.

Ensuring Quality and Accessibility
Therefore, policy frameworks must ensure the high quality of these technologies and make them universally accessible to benefit the educational sphere. This ranges from providing the needed infrastructure in underprivileged areas to benchmarking AI educational tools by which they shall show proficiency in meeting instructional needs.

Fostering Training and Professional Development
A practical policy framework would encourage comprehensive training programs for educators that equip them to use AI tools effectively in teaching, understand their possibilities and upcoming challenges, and identify strategic ways to use them to improve students' learning.

Promoting Innovation and Research
Therefore, policy frameworks must encourage research and development to improve further and innovate educational AI. This, in turn, will involve funding and building up synergies between academic institutions, tech companies, and policymakers. The other salient dimension to developing further advanced and fairer educational AI tools is fostering innovation through policy initiatives.

This forms the basis of policy frameworks for AI in education about complex realities. This underscores an approach that needs to be navigated regarding considerations of quality and accessibility, which play a pivotal role in tapping AI's potential on the educational landscape in an all-inclusive manner.

Fostering a Culture of Innovation and Continuous Learning

We live in a world of rapid technological change and interconnectedness that requires talent for innovation and embracing lifelong learning for personal and professional development. This point can arguably find no better relevance than in the introductory undergraduate educational system, where instilling a culture of innovativeness and continuous learning can help prepare students for the necessary skills required by a world of change and complexity.

The Need for Innovation and Continuous Learning
For undergraduate education, innovation involves developing new ideas, products, and processes and an open mentality for exploring the undiscovered and change. This works congruently with continuous learning to create a life practice of knowledge-based living and application, which goes beyond the four walls of a classroom.

These are competencies that no student can afford not to be part of his education because they will form the basis of his potential to fit and grow in such a dynamic global backdrop of technological progression and societal shifts.

Innovation, introducing something new or improving the current idea, catalyses growth and development across sectors—if anything. From the steam engine during the Industrial Revolution to the most modern digital revolution spurred by the internet, innovation has been the pulse of progress among societies and economies.

These improve efficiency and productivity in dealing with significant challenges such as climate change, health crises, and social inequality. For example, renewable energy technologies, such as solar and wind power, provide sustainable options for fossil fuels to mitigate the impact of climate change.

Similarly, significant advances in medical technology, such as mRNA vaccines, have been used to respond very quickly to international health crises. Not just the future of breakthrough technologies but an imagination of what could be and realisation—the transformation in new ways for sustainable problem-solving to uplift life and lead towards co-creating a just and sustainable future for all.

In today's fast-moving world, change is the only constant. Because of this, continued learning is the only subject in which people continue to expand their knowledge and skills throughout their lives. Eventually, continuous learning is essential to an individual's personal and professional success.

At the professional level, this further helps in increasing employability since new skills and knowledge develop an individual's competitive and adaptive character within a dynamically changing job market.

For example, rapid growth in artificial intelligence and automation indicates that the future will require more developed problem-solving skills and emotional intelligence. Specifically, lifelong learning is one of the things that makes my life much more fulfilled and enriched. It fosters curiosity, improves self-esteem, and encourages an active and engaged mind.

Another call for continuous learning comes from innovation. Learning lays the basis for creative thinking and problem-solving, whereby a person or an organisation can develop new ideas or ways of doing things.
Organisations cultivating a learning culture using their workforce's collective knowledge and creativity bring more effective innovation. For example, companies such as Google and 3M give employees time to work on personal projects and learn; some of the most innovative products and services come from this.

Current Educational Practices and Challenges
A culture that celebrates creativity, critical thinking, and adaptability cannot be developed through traditional education models, which rely on rote learning and standardised testing.

This gap reflects the need for educational reform, which is reasonably needed to impart knowledge, develop students' passions as lifelong learners, and innovate.

Despite these significant advantages, it is full of challenges that stand in the way of innovation and continuous learning. These include the most critical impediments to resistance to change, both from individuals and organisational comfort zones of the routines often like safe harbours, and if anything, view new ideas or technologies with scepticism.

This inclination results in resistance, which discourages the adoption of innovative solutions and chokes creativity.

Above and beyond, the massive challenge of digital division brings. In this manner, the "digital divide" can further strengthen all the current disparities by preventing access to participation in the digital economy and educational resources for specific populations.
Part of the problem also emanates from the educational systems in many countries. They must adequately prepare the students for the workforce, which changes quickly. Old-style education often tends toward learning by rote and standardised examination rather than accenting critical thought and imagination—acquiring skills required for innovation and agility.

Individuals and organisations alike can devise many strategies to overcome these challenges. The most important of these is inculcating a culture of curiosity and receptivity to new ideas, which can be initiated through policies encouraging taking risks and learning from failures rather than punishing them. With a growth mindset, one sees many significant opportunities to learn and grow from challenges.

Organisational investment in training and development programs helps employees upgrade and change with new technologies and methodologies. Governments and educational institutions working in collaboration should reform the education systems to ensure critical thinking, creativity, and digital literacy, preparing children for tomorrow.

Strategies for Fostering Innovation and Learning
This is possible through redesigning the corona, emphasising interdisciplinary learning and problem-solving in real-world situations. Pedagogical strategies should enable an upper hand in experiential activities like internships, research projects, and collaborative activities in such a way that students can apply into practice the theoretical knowledge that has previously been obtained. In addition, the institution could better support the learning environment with resources, spaces, and programs needed to be more innovative.

Examples of Successful Implementation

Institutions like MIT and Stanford are leading the way in this. They are known for relentless innovation and lifelong learning via best-in-class research opportunities and project-based courses within the undergraduate experience, coupled with a dizzying array of entrepreneurship programs. These are universities that other institutions can look up to so that they may do the same within their communities.

With this brief background, we shall now illustrate a few examples of actual institutions applying these principles in practice to further our discussion on the culture of fostering innovation and continuous learning. Such examples will reveal strategies and results showing how organisations establish excellent environments for employees to engage in practices linked with innovation and life learning.

1. Google: Embracing Innovation through Employee Empowerment

Google has become a paragon of innovation because of its bold corporate culture that exerts and encourages creativity and even audacity in experimentation. Another practice this company has been known to do is the "20% time," in which employees can take one day each week to work on exciting projects that may not necessarily be related to their usual jobs. This policy is what has seen some of Google's most successful products like Gmail and Google News.

In addition, Google spends a lot on employee development through continuous training programs and workshops in machine learning, coding, and leadership. By doing these two, Google maintains the position of technology leadership and remains the most preferred workplace: innovation-driven by employees and continuous education.

2. Massachusetts Institute of Technology (MIT): A Hub for Continuous Learning and Innovation

MIT stands as a perfect example of how educational institutions could well be institutions to promote the culture of continuous learning and fostering innovation. The open courseware initiative at MIT offers an array of open access to course materials across disciplines, giving learners worldwide a chance to explore new areas of knowledge.

Besides being one of the most interdisciplinary, world-renowned research labs, the Media Lab at MIT brings students and researchers from many fields together to tackle projects ranging from technology to multimedia, sciences, art, and design. This approach delivers a path-breaking innovation and inculcates the spirit of lifelong learning and cross-disciplinary collaboration among the participants.

3. 3M: Cultivating Innovation through Freedom to Explore

A worldwide conglomerate known for innovation, 3 M's success has been attributed to a culture that allows employees to explore and experiment. Much like Google's "20% Time, "15% Culture" at 3M enables employees to use some of their work time to decide on project ideas, hence developing a creative and experimenting environment.

With this policy, many products, like Post-it Notes, were born. Moreover, 3M invests in lifelong learning by providing training and development resources to its employees, thus allowing them opportunities for innovation and career development growth.

4. Khan Academy: Promoting Continuous Learning through Accessible Education

Khan Academy is a non-profit educational organisation whose mission is to provide a world-class education for free to anyone, anywhere. With its library of thousands of tutorials and exercises in subjects ranging from math to the humanities, Khan Academy empowers people of all ages to learn.

Therefore, the platform has made the learning process more interesting through gamification and has motivated learners to set and meet goals. Khan Academy is one of the few examples in the world whereby we observe how technology makes the vision of democratising education and fostering a global culture of lifelong learning possible.

These examples illustrate diverse approaches to fostering innovation and continuous learning across sectors. From motivating their employees with passion projects or interdisciplinary character research environments to an atmosphere of training and development or democratising education with the help of technology, these institutions illustrate the benefits of encouraging culture towards improvement and creative processes.

This can also help other organisations that would like to do the same in their setup, which means the knowledge from this example is generic for encouraging innovations and lifelong learning.

Teaching an innovative and lifelong learning spirit among students during their undergraduate years is necessary. In other words, universities have to follow a holistic approach and reorient old curricula, modes of teaching, and institutional support systems so that students are geared up and ready to take on the future.

CHAPTER 9

Global Perspectives of AI in Education

Comparative Analysis of AI Adoption in Education Across Different Countries

Conducting a critical comparative analysis of the adoption of AI in education globally will require considering factors such as the level of technology integration, policy framework in place, investment, challenges faced, and, finally, the outcomes. The following section will analyse four countries with diversified approaches to AI in education: the United States, China, Finland, and India. We zeroed in on these countries because they have diversified educational policies, and not all of them are at the same level regarding technology development and the strategic focus on AI.

United States: Leading in Innovation and Private Sector Collaboration

When it comes to education, a transparent collaboration between the education sector and private technological companies is required to make innovation possible in the country. American universities and tech companies are at the forefront of advancing this push to AI in personalised learning, automation of administrative tasks, and increased research capabilities.

However, in the U.S.' decentralised education system, the integration of AI varies from state to state and, most often, from institution to institution, contingent mainly on funding and local policy. This includes using AI even in learning institutions other than the conventional set-up, hence an initiative such as the Next Generation Food Systems AI Institute.

China: State-Driven Ambition and Comprehensive Integration

China has a very strategic and state-driven approach to AI in education, with the government setting ambitious goals to become the world leader in AI, including applications in the educational sector, by 2030. Significant investment is made into infrastructure, research, and development, focusing on developing intelligent classrooms, AI-based tutoring systems, and educational platforms.

This stands in contrast to the United States, where national standards and significant critical government investments have propounded a more equitable spread of AI integrations nationwide. China's education system emphasises using AI to enhance learning outcomes and monitor students' progress and behaviour.

Finland: Focus on Ethical AI and Equitable Education

Finland is world-renewed for having one of the most qualitative education systems, if not the best globally. It has approached AI with peculiar heed to ethics, equity, and lifelong learning. They guide the development and use of AI. The Finnish government encourages the use of technology. It ensures support so that it is a tool for the teachers and students to harness learning, not replace conventional ways.

Programs like the AI Education Program are meant to provide its citizenry with skills to use AI effectively, wherein critical thinking and digital literacy are extensively featured. A holistically approached program from Finland will ensure that the implementation of AI does not facilitate the widening of the gap between those who have access to quality education and those who do not but instead supports inclusive education.

India: Rapid Growth with Challenges in Access and Infrastructure

A case in point is India, where AI adaptation in education is increasing and inspired by government initiatives and private enterprises. Therefore, a set of challenges before the country is equitable access for such an extensive and diverse population and infrastructure to be made available to break these barriers.

On the one hand, the government undertook initiatives like AI For All, conceived to take AI knowledge and tools to every student and educator, and teemed for benefits. However, a major stumbling block lies under the umbrella of the digital divide, as in most cases, the rural backdrop needs access to the resources and adequate connectivity to have a full impact on AI in education.

Aspect	United States	China	Finland	India
Policy Framework	Decentralised, with significant private sector involvement.	Centralised and strategic, with substantial state direction and funding.	Ethical and equitable, with a focus on enhancing traditional education.	Growing, with efforts to democratise AI knowledge across diverse populations.
Level of Integration	High in specific institutions and states.	Comprehensive, with national standards.	Selective, with an emphasis on supporting education rather than replacing it.	Rapidly growing but uneven due to access and infrastructure challenges.
Challenges	Varied levels of integration and access.	Privacy concerns and over-monitoring.	Ensuring AI supports rather than overshadows traditional methods.	Digital divide and infrastructure limitations.
Outcomes	Innovation in personalised learning and administrative automation.	Enhanced learning outcomes and efficient monitoring of student progress.	A balanced approach to AI, maintaining high educational standards and inclusivity.	Increased access to educational resources, with ongoing efforts to bridge the digital divide.

This study of comparative nature, therefore, mirrors the different strategies and AI outcomes in education adaptation by other countries. The United States and China lead in AI technology, but their policies and integration modes are divergent. Finland is built around technologies with great respect for ethics and equity consideration, ensuring they complement the education system.

On the other hand, India's unique challenges have been due to its scale and diversity.

Access to education primarily focuses on using AI to enhance quality for its ever-growing population.

Each country's experiences show valuable lessons regarding the potential benefits and pitfalls of integrating AI into educational frameworks, with apparent needs for context-specific and need-based approaches.

Success Stories and Lessons Learned

Promises and Implications, quoted in Global Perspectives on AI in Education, "shows a rich tapestry of cases from around the world that both paint success stories and give essential lessons for guiding future implementations of AI technologies in education. Observing some prominent world examples, one can make over the strategies that bring successful outcomes and the challenges to tap its potential so that AI becomes helpful in education.

Success Stories
Singapore: Nurturing Future-Ready Learners On the one hand, the former Singapore infuses AI literacy and skills in the curriculum to prepare its students for the changing world. The country has introduced AI-driven platforms like Squirrel AI, which helps to personalise student learning by attuning to their pace and style of learning. It is this kind son: "This holistic use of technology, strongly emphasising ethically critical values, has underpinned Singapore's success. As already seen, the ability to prepare teachers with efficient AI tools is critical. If AI is to be successfully implemented within the education system, then stakeholders will need a workable cadre of professionals.

United Arab Emirates (UAE): Leading Innovation in the Arab World That's why the UAE has become the leader in AI education among Middle Eastern countries. As part of the Mohammed Bin Rashid Al Maktoum Global Initiatives, none of the projects could be AI customisation of learning and improvements in educational achievements.

One example is Alef Education, an AI-powered, machine-learning platform deployed in UAE schools that offers students a customised approach to learning mathematics and science. The platform's success demonstrates the importance of aligning AI tools with educational goals to enhance learning.

Lessons Learned
Inclusivity and Equity One of the paramount lessons from the global implementations of AI in education is the critical importance that must be emphasised to ensure inclusivity and equity. The projects in India and Africa brought to the forefront the idea that there could be an added element of risk for greater inclusion linked to AI: educational inequality that may ensue from uneven technological access.

Addressing this will mean that all efforts need strategies targeting the enrolment of the underprivileged and rural students, thereby ensuring that the other 80% of the students benefit from the implementation of AI and not just the well-resourced background students.

Data Privacy and Ethical Concerns
Its use in education has raised eyebrows over data privacy and ethics issues. Finland and Germany are some of the countries at the frontier with stringent regulations regarding data protection and ethics in the use of AI. This calls again for transparent policies to ensure that the information is safeguarded and the AI tools are not abused.

Teacher Empowerment Another vital lesson is that teachers should be empowered during AI integration. Indeed, Singapore and South Korea's experiences, as successful stories with the right kind of training and resources at teachers' disposal, demonstrate how their application of AI tools to the teaching process can enhance the learning experience without feeling threatened by technology.

Teacher empowerment in this domain includes technical and pedagogical assistance to educators that helps them integrate AI methods to complement and enhance traditional pedagogical methods.

Continuous Evaluation and Adaptation
AI technology's dynamic nature and diversity in educational contexts call for continual evaluation and adaptation of the AI tool. This calls for setting feedback mechanisms to the impact of AI on learning outcomes and student engagement, hence allowing adjustments and improvements with time.

The development is iterative, which Estonia's digital education strategy tries to facilitate to avoid having a Global Perspective. The review provides AI in education from a global point of view, presenting different ways, problems, and achievements, starting from the advanced Singapore curriculum to the invaluable country's experience in AI innovation of platforms in the UAE.

Critical lessons in inclusivity, privacy, empowerment of the teacher, and the need for constant change provide signposts along the way for future implementations of AI in education. Countries should use these principles to guide the murky waters of the implementation of AI in their education systems as they move toward solutions that will enhance learning experiences and, at the same time, not compromise, if possible, improve any of the ethical and practical challenges.

International Collaboration and Policy Development

Leading collaboration and policy development between countries, however, will be to ensure that the potential of AI in education is met. This sharing will likely enable countries to pool their knowledge, resources, and best practices to ensure that adopting AI technologies benefits learners across the globe. That is bound to ensure the fair deployment of AI in education, considering responsible and effective deployment of the technologies. Let's explore further what international collaboration and policy development stand for in AI for education.

International Collaboration: Bridging Gaps and Sharing Insights

UNESCO's Role in Facilitating Global Standards

The United Nations Educational, Scientific, and Cultural Organization (UNESCO) leads international cooperation with AI in education. Through worldwide standards and ethical guidance, the organisation fosters an environment in which AI tools will promote access to quality education by all students from an inclusive and equitable point of view. For instance, the Beijing Consensus for AI and Education provides guidelines or principles for using AI in education that focus on equitable access and protecting learners' privacy.

- *Global Partnerships and Initiatives:* International partnerships—like the Global Education A Coalition recently launched by UNESCO, which brings governments, NGOs, and the private sector together on AI education projects, can enable countries to share state-of-the-art solutions and technologies to support and guide them in effectively integrating AI to solve educational challenges, paying particular attention to underserved communities. Such a collaborative research approach would enable the establishment of new AI technologies that may find their applicability in various educational scenarios.

Policy Development: Creating Frameworks for Responsible AI Use

- *National AI Education Policies:* Many more countries fully appreciate the importance of national policies to guide the integration of AI within comprehensive educational systems. The policies have recently focused on infrastructure development, teacher training, curriculum adaptation, and ethical considerations. South Korea's AI Education Strategy, for instance, includes plans to reflect AI in the state curriculum, training for teachers, and elaboration of school-based ethical guidelines regarding the use of AI.

• *International Policy Coordination:* Therefore, excellent coordination will be required among various international bodies to develop cohesive policies that may best target AI's global educational challenges. On the other hand, efforts are underway to establish international policy frameworks that would see a united front on ethical issues, data privacy, and the proportionate use of AI. Coordination thereof will ensure that there are no disparities in adopting the innovation across regions or backgrounds so that the learners in such jurisdictions benefit from educational innovations.

• *Challenges and Opportunities:* Despite the potential benefits, international collaboration and policy development in AI education face several challenges. They could be at the regulation level of the environments that might diverge, differences at the infrastructure level, or differences in priorities militating against the harmonisation of efforts; however, such challenges present themselves as opportunities to learn and adapt. When addressed through international collaborations, such differences may bring about holistic solutions that consider local contexts and benefit from global perspectives.

Moving Forward

To ensure that the following are considered among the primary focuses for stakeholders in international collaboration and policy development to maximise the potential benefits of AI in education:

- Aligning ethical standards to ensure the responsible use of AI in education.
- Sharing best practices and resources to support countries at different stages of AI adoption.
- Investing in research and development to innovate and adapt AI technologies for education.
- Prioritising teacher and educator training to integrate AI tools effectively into teaching and learning processes.

The global coordination road of AI approaches in education is strewn with complex challenges but leads toward great educational dividends in equity, quality, and innovation. AI technology promises to transform learners' accessible, personal, and practical learning approach through global collaboration and cohesive policies.

It highlights that international collaboration at the level of AI in education and policy-making are two vital elements that will help unleash AI's full potential to change learning outcomes worldwide. Such collaboration shall be meant for best practices, innovations, and ethical conduct that ensure technology is employed for the good of learners within varied contexts. This methodology will help respond to general concerns ranging from assuring equal access to AI resources to addressing the privacy and security of data.

The Role of International Collaboration
International AI education cooperation involves various activities, such as joint research projects, policy dialogues, and global initiatives. These may take the following forms:
- *Standardising Ethics Guidelines*: Organisations such as UNESCO and OECD have been leading international efforts to develop common international principles for the ethical use of AI in education. These guidelines centre on four primary dimensions: equity, inclusiveness, transparency, and accountability, with national policy frameworks.

• *Sharing the Best of Innovation:* Websites such as AI in Education Society afford to share innovative best practices in teaching and AI applications that enable educators and policymakers to learn from successful implementation in other countries.

• *Develop Open Educational Resources (OERs):* Collaboration can enable the development of OERs, which include openly available, licensed text, media, and other digital assets used in teaching, learning, and research. This is further adaptable through AI and can be delivered according to local needs to make quality education more obtainable.

• *Capacity building:* Most international cooperation in the capacity development of low—and middle-income countries addresses this issue. Such collaborations can help bridge the digital divide and serve the cause of global equity in education by training educators and sharing AI tools and infrastructures.

Policy Development for AI in Education
Policies need to be developed about AI in education, which is significant while integrating this technology with thought and ethics into learning environments. Effective policy frameworks need to understand the following key areas:

Privacy and Data Protection: Policies are needed in learning data protection with explicit mention of ways data collection, storage, handling, and sharing are to be executed. The European General Data Protection Regulation (GDPR) provides a powerful model for personal data protection within educational facilities.

• *Equity and Access:* Policies should ensure that AI tools and resources are accessible to all students equally, including those from marginalised communities and differently-abled students. To ensure that AI reaches out to all sections, especially the vulnerable ones, its application in education should not segregate

them further. It should not be a source of bias or inequality.
• *Quality and accountability*: Standards need to be set for the quality of AI-driven educational content and tools, taking utmost care that they are pedagogically sound, which improves learning outcomes. Mechanisms for accountability to measure and report the impact of AI in education need to be implemented.

• *Teacher Preparation and Support*: Effective in-service AI teacher preparation and support must be provided to prepare the teachers effectively and make them confident in the teaching-learning transaction.
• *Innovation and Research:* Lastly, innovation and research in AI education need to be a focus of policy frameworks through funding of pilot projects. For example, research on the long-term effect of AI on learning and new pedagogical approaches needs to be developed.

International cooperation and working together on how best to use AI for solid education across the globe should lay. The countries will not only be in a position to share knowledge and challenges, but they will also put in place an education system that prepares every learner for the future.

In the same way, a policy focused on issues of equity, privacy, and quality would guarantee that AI integration in education works for the betterment of learning outcomes, teacher support, and general educational experiences.

CHAPTER 10

Ethical and Social Implications of AI in Education

Integrating Artificial Intelligence (AI) in education brings myriad ethical and social implications that require careful consideration. As AI technologies become increasingly prevalent in learning environments, from primary schools to universities and beyond, stakeholders must navigate the potential benefits while addressing these technologies' complex challenges. These implications touch on privacy, equity, the role of teachers, and the nature of learning itself.

Privacy and Data Security
One of the most pressing ethical concerns is the management of student data. AI systems rely on vast data to personalise learning, assess student progress, and predict future performance. This raises significant questions about privacy, consent, and data security. There is a risk that sensitive information could be misused, leading to breaches of confidentiality or the unauthorised sharing of personal data. Ensuring robust data protection measures and transparent data policies is crucial to safeguard student privacy.

Integrating Artificial Intelligence (AI) into educational systems has opened many opportunities for enhancing learning experiences and operational efficiency. However, this technological evolution brings significant ethical challenges concerning privacy and data security. As educational institutions increasingly rely on AI for personalised learning, assessment tools, and administrative automation, collecting and processing vast amounts of sensitive student information become inevitable. Ensuring the ethical management of this data is paramount, necessitating a comprehensive approach to privacy and data security.

The primary concern revolves around the transparent and consensual collection of data. Students or their guardians for minors must be fully informed about what data is being collected, its intended use, and how it will be stored and shared. This transparency is the cornerstone of trust in educational technologies. Moreover, the security of data storage systems against unauthorised access is crucial. This includes external threats such as cyber-attacks and internal vulnerabilities like unauthorised staff access.

An equally pressing issue is the potential for AI systems to perpetuate or even exacerbate biases present in their training data, leading to discriminatory outcomes against specific student demographics. Addressing these biases is crucial for ensuring the equitable use of AI in educational settings.

To navigate these ethical challenges, several strategies can be employed:

- **Adopting Robust Data Protection Policies**: Institutions must develop and enforce strong data protection policies that align with legal standards like the GDPR in the EU or COPPA in the US. These policies should clearly define data collection, storage, use, and sharing practices.

- **Establishing Ethical AI Guidelines**: Beyond legal compliance, creating ethical guidelines for AI use can further safeguard privacy and security. These guidelines should prioritise the welfare of students and ensure that educational objectives are at the forefront of AI deployment.

- **Strengthening Cybersecurity Measures**: Implementing advanced cybersecurity measures, including encryption and secure authentication, is essential for protecting against data breaches. Institutions should also have incident response strategies ready for potential data security breaches.

- **Ensuring Transparency and Accountability**: Transparency about AI use and its data security measures fosters trust. Educational entities should be aware of their AI technologies and take responsibility for any privacy infringements or data misuse.

- **Involving the Educational Community**: The development and evaluation of AI technologies should include input from educators and students. Their perspectives are invaluable in identifying privacy concerns and guiding the ethical development of AI tools.

- **Conducting Regular Monitoring and Evaluations**: Ongoing oversight of AI systems is necessary to identify and mitigate emerging privacy and security issues. This includes reassessing AI's impact on student privacy and adapting data protection practices as needed.

While AI presents transformative potential for education, navigating the ethical landscape of privacy and data security is crucial. Through proactive measures, transparent practices, and inclusive policymaking, educational institutions can leverage AI to enrich learning while steadfastly protecting students' privacy and data security.

Equity and Accessibility
The promise of AI in education is to provide personalised learning experiences that can adapt to the individual needs of

each student, potentially levelling the playing field for those whom traditional educational models may disadvantage. However, there exists a significant risk that AI could exacerbate existing inequalities. Access to the necessary technology and digital infrastructure is not uniform across different socio-economic groups and geographical areas. Moreover, AI systems can inherit biases present in their training data or the assumptions of their developers, leading to outcomes that unfairly disadvantage certain groups of students.

The Role of Teachers
The advent of AI in education also prompts a re-evaluation of the role of teachers. While AI can automate specific tasks, such as grading and even some aspects of personalised instruction, it cannot replace the essential human elements of teaching, including empathy, moral guidance, and the fostering of social skills. There is a concern that over-reliance on AI could devalue these aspects of education, leading to a diminished role for teachers and potentially a depersonalised learning experience for students.

Transforming the Nature of Learning
AI has the potential to fundamentally change the nature of learning, making education more flexible, interactive, and tailored to individual interests and needs. However, this shift also raises questions about the standardisation of knowledge and the development of critical thinking skills. There's a delicate balance between providing personalised learning paths and ensuring a comprehensive education that exposes students to diverse viewpoints and areas of knowledge.

Ethical Development and Deployment of AI
The development and deployment of AI in education must be guided by ethical principles that prioritise students' well-being, autonomy, and rights. This includes the responsible design of AI systems to avoid biases, the involvement of educators and students in the development process, and ongoing monitoring to

assess the impact of AI on educational outcomes and social equality.

The ethical and social implications of AI in education are vast and complex. A multi-stakeholder approach involving educators, policymakers, technologists, and the broader community is essential to navigate these challenges. By prioritising ethical considerations and social equity, integrating AI into education can fulfil its potential to enhance learning outcomes, make education more inclusive, and prepare students for a future in which technology and human collaboration are increasingly intertwined.

Addressing Bias in AI Algorithms
The burgeoning use of Artificial Intelligence (AI) in education can revolutionise how we teach, learn, and manage educational institutions. However, the excitement surrounding these possibilities is tempered by recognising a significant challenge: the risk of bias in AI algorithms. This bias can skew educational content, assessments, and administrative decisions, potentially reinforcing societal inequalities. Addressing bias in AI algorithms is thus not just a technical hurdle but a fundamental ethical concern, crucial for ensuring that AI technologies support equitable and inclusive education.

Bias in AI can manifest in various forms, affecting individuals based on race, gender, socioeconomic status, disability, and more. Such biases, often reflecting historical data and societal inequalities, can lead to unfair treatment of students, misrepresentations in educational content, and biased assessments. The repercussions profoundly impact students' educational experiences, outcomes, and perceptions of their potential. Consequently, mitigating bias in AI within the academic sector is imperative to harness AI's benefits fairly and responsibly.

Ensuring Diverse and Representative Data

A critical step in combating AI bias is utilising diverse and representative data sets for training AI algorithms. These data sets must encompass various student demographics, including different ethnicities, genders, abilities, and socioeconomic backgrounds. By training AI systems with diverse data, developers can create more generalisable and equitable algorithms in their applications, minimising the risk of biased outcomes.

Promoting Algorithmic Transparency

Transparency in AI algorithm design is essential for understanding decisions, particularly in educational contexts where these decisions can significantly impact students' lives. Explainable AI (XAI) approaches aim to make the inner workings of AI models more understandable to humans, enabling educators, students, and policymakers to scrutinise and trust AI-driven processes.

Implementing Regular Audits and Bias Testing

Continuous monitoring for bias through regular audits and testing is vital to identify and rectify biases in AI algorithms. Independent evaluations should assess algorithm performance across diverse demographic groups, pinpointing disparities. Such proactive measures ensure biases are addressed promptly, maintaining the integrity and fairness of AI applications in education.

Involving Diverse Perspectives in AI Development

Incorporating a broad spectrum of perspectives in developing and deploying AI technologies can significantly mitigate bias. This approach involves engaging educators, students, and communities from varied backgrounds in the design and evaluation processes. Their input can guide the development of inclusive AI tools that meet the diverse needs of the student population.

Adhering to Ethical AI Guidelines

Establishing and following ethical guidelines for using AI in education is crucial. These guidelines should emphasise fairness, equity, and the well-being of students, serving as a cornerstone for the responsible use of AI technologies. They highlight the importance of avoiding harm and ensuring that AI-driven innovations benefit all students equally.

Educating Stakeholders on AI Ethics

Finally, educating educators, administrators, and policymakers about the potential for bias in AI and the ethical considerations of using AI tools is essential. This education can empower them to make informed decisions about integrating AI into educational settings, recognising its limitations and potential.

Addressing the challenge of bias in AI algorithms within the education sector requires a multifaceted approach. These strategies encompass the development of diverse data sets, promoting algorithmic transparency, regular bias audits, inclusive development processes, adherence to ethical guidelines, and comprehensive stakeholder education. By undertaking these strategies, the educational community can ensure that AI technologies offer equitable, inclusive, and empowering learning experiences, leveraging AI's transformative potential responsibly and justly.

Addressing Bias in AI Algorithms

Integrating Artificial Intelligence (AI) into education presents several issues that must be considered, including ethical and social implications. The fact that AI technologies penetrate learning environments—from primary schools to universities and even further—means that stakeholders will find their way around the possibilities and opportunities offered by these technologies. However, they will have to deal with serious challenges that they pose. These implications touch on privacy, equity, the role of teachers, and the nature of learning itself.

Privacy and Data Security

The great concern is the data management of student records, and more so is ethics. AI systems need enormous amounts of data to be able to give a personalised learning experience, the progress of students, and predict performance in the future. This, therefore, poses pertinent privacy, consent, and data security questions. However, the most significant risks would be any sensitive information leak that could jeopardise the institution's security policies, the confidentiality of the subjects, or the sharing of personal data with unauthorised people. The student's privacy rights should be ensured through solid data protection and clear data policies.

The entry of Artificial Intelligence (AI) into educational systems opens innumerable avenues for bettering learning experience and operational efficiency. However, technological evolution is associated with major ethical issues, especially privacy and data security. With the increased role of AI in personalised learning, assessment tools, and administrative automation, sensitive information about students will be collected and, in any manner, processed. The sole concern is that if the management is ethical, it requires a complete circle around privacy and data security considerations.

In reality, the stake is the transparent and consensual collection of data on various contents: the students' data, their purposes, the type of data collected, and how information is stored and distributed to students or their guardians when the students are minors. This transparency is the basis of trust in educational technologies. The data system for their storage should also be secure from access by a third person, including external threats, such as cyber-attacks, and the ones from the inside, for example, unauthorised access by staff.

It is just as pressing, then, that AI systems have the potential to further encourage biases in their training data and thus result in an even more discriminatory outcome against specific student demographics. The centrality here is the need to redress such biases to ensure that educational settings use AI equitably.

Several strategies can be employed to navigate these ethical challenges: Strong Data Protection Policies: Strong policies need to be developed for data protection in institutions, conforming to the standards set by law, such as the General Data Protection Regulation in the EU and COPPA in the USA. Properly defined institutional policies exist for data collection, storage, use, and sharing practices.

Set Ethical AI Guidelines: In addition to legal compliance, establish ethically fair guidelines for using AI, such that the tools do not infringe upon privacy and security. To this end, the guidelines should ensure that student benefit is at the forefront and prioritise ensuring that the system's deployment does not come at the cost of the educational goal.

Strengthening Cyber Security Measures: Advanced protection, including encryption and secure authentication, should be deployed to avoid these kinds of breaches. They should also be prepared with incident response strategies in case of any potential risk to data security.

Ensuring Transparency and Accountability: Transparency in AI and data security builds trust. Educational entities should be willing to share information about their AI technologies and be mindful of any privacy violations or data abuse.

Engaging the academic community: AI technology development and evaluation shall be done in consultation with educators and students. This will help them identify the privacy issues associated with AI tools and may help guide their ethical development.

Regular monitoring and evaluation are conducted, which means that the periodic checking and controlling of the AI systems are needed to be vigilant about any privacy and security issues that may occur. They must reassess their influence over student privacy and adapt their data protection methods.

Although AI offers transformational potential to education, treading the ethical landscape on privacy and data security is paramount. Hence, educational institutions can continue to use AI for better learning but with a focus on two aspects: the necessity of proactive measures and the transparency of practices, along with inclusive policy-making regarding students' privacy and data security.

Equity and Accessibility

Artificial intelligence promises a learning experience that is tailor-made for a student. It will adapt to that particular student's specific needs and thus be a great equaliser for those for whom an education modelled for one size would be disadvantaged. However, it has a high potential for aggravating existing inequalities since the required technology and digital infrastructure are homogeneously unavailable in different socio-economic groups and geographical areas. Additionally, AI systems can learn biases from the training data used or be designed with the biases of their developers, thereby producing outcomes that would unfairly disadvantage certain groups of students.

The Role of Teachers
The advent of AI in education also prompts a re-evaluation of the role of teachers. Although AI does have the potential to automate tasks such as grading up to a certain point and thereby make it almost personalised, it still does not have the replaceable value for the essential teaching aspects requiring human intervention, such as empathy, moral guidance, and fostering social skills. However, it is a concern that these elements of learning might become devalued in some way if there is too much reliance on AI, and therefore, the role of the teacher might be diminished, even though the teacher will remain integral to the whole process in one form or another.

Transforming the Nature of Learning
AI promises to change very many natures of learning, making it more flexible, interactive, and customised to individual interests and needs. On the other side of the scale-shifting paradigm, questions and issues border on knowledge standardisation and building critical thinking skills. Hence comes the delicate balance—personalised learning paths versus education that build towards being eclectic in perspectives and bodies of knowledge.

Ethical Development and Deployment of AI
If AI is to be developed and implemented in educational practice, it must be done through the students' well-being, autonomy, and

rights. This would include the responsible design of an AI system against bias, engagement with educators and students in its development, and continued monitoring of the same to measure its effects on educational outcomes and social equality.

AI's ethical and social implications in education are immense and complex. It is the most viable solution to these challenges if, and only if, a multi-stakeholder approach that effectively mobilises educators, policymakers, technologists, and the larger community to grapple with them is instituted and empowered.

Summarising:

Considering all these basics, ethical considerations, and social equity, the integration of AI in education might leverage its capacity to enhance learning outcomes, make this sector more inclusive, and prepare students for future needs, where technology and human collaboration would be more entertained.

Addressing Bias in AI Algorithms The booming use of Artificial Intelligence (AI) in education may transform how institutions teach, students learn and administer educational affairs. But, in a way, the excitement for this potential was dampened by the realisation of a significant challenge: the risk of biased AI algorithms.

It may be this bias through which the learning content, assessments, and administrative decisions are skewed, thereby reinforcing societal inequality. In this regard, AI algorithms and their related biases present a technical and central ethical concern for society if AI technologies are to be harnessed to support the vision of equitable and inclusive education.

Other severe and harmful forms of bias may be less frequent, but the fact that they could feature in AI pertains to race, gender, socio-economic status, disability, and so forth. Typically, instances of such biases reflect historical data and social disparities. This may lead to unfair treatment among students, expressly misrepresenting educational content and biased assessment.

The student's educational experiences, outcomes, and self-perception of their potential are drenched under such consequences. Dealing with this problem becomes critical to the fruits of AI being leveraged justly and responsibly.

Ensuring Diverse and Representative Data It is recommended that one of the fundamental ways to counter AI bias is through diverse and representative sets of data used in the training of AI algorithms. All are included in representations of different student bodies across various ethnicities, genders, abilities, and socio-economic statuses.

This guides developers in creating fairer and generally applicable algorithms in the implementation, reducing the risk of bias in outcomes.

Promoting Algorithmic Transparency
Of particular interest in the educational context is the transparency of the design of the AI algorithms, helping to understand such decisions, as these can have colossal effects on students' lives.

Explainable AI (XAI) approaches endeavour to provide the means to make AI model predictions interpretable to human users, which is paramount for educators, students, and policy-makers to be able to look into and trust the processes that AI is running.

Implementing Regular Audits and Bias Testing
Regular audits and testing must be followed to monitor bias, and when bias is found in the AI algorithms, it must be fixed. Under independent evaluations, the algorithmic performance will be tested for disparities among different demographic groups. Such proactive measures ensure that biases are addressed as and when needed to retain the AI applications' integrity and fairness.

Involving Diverse Perspectives in AI Development, a Broad variation of views concerning the development and deployment of AI technology could notably minimise bias. This approach includes lecturers, students, and community members in the design and appraisal processes.

Their input can guide the development of inclusive AI tools that meet the diverse needs of the student population.

Adhering to Ethical AI Guidelines
It becomes essential to stipulate and follow ethical guidelines when using AI in education. This will underscore that the students' fairness, equity, and well-being are crucial to responsible usage of AI technology. These essentially point out the need to ensure no harm and, for that matter, guarantee that AI-powered innovations accrue benefits to every student equally.

Educating Stakeholders on AI Ethics
In the end, educators, administrators, and policy advocates must be exposed to the possibility of AI bias and some ethical considerations associated with implementing AI tools. Such education can help them make effective and informed decisions about incorporating AI in educational settings, knowing its boundaries and potential.

This would thus call for a multi-pronged approach to AI algorithms in the education sector, as discussed above. These would combine diverse data sets, algorithmic transparency, audits for bias, and highly inclusive and ethical development processes with stakeholder education.

Social Responsibility and AI

The novelty brought by artificial intelligence (AI) in the education world changes, in fact, the way of organising learning contexts, the mode of presenting didactic material, and the perception regarding student involvement and preparedness. The potential of this technological revolution—in fact, to further fundamentally improve access and effectiveness in education—is loaded with commensurate complex ethical challenges and social responsibilities. That means AI integration in education contributes positively toward the learning experience of thoroughly understanding roles and coming together efforts to work on them.

Ensuring Equitable Access and Outcomes

In other words, the promise that learning will be personalised and that quality education will become available to all lies in equal access to such technologies. Therefore, this social responsibility needs to reflect active work to break down barriers that deny the benefit of AI in education to specific groups. This social responsibility, thus, needs to reflect active work in the dismantling of barriers that deny specific groups the benefits of AI in education, which include:

Bridging the Digital Divide: Policies and initiatives must be implemented to ensure that all students have an equal opportunity to access the necessary digital tools and the Internet so that learning enhanced through AI does not become a privilege seen to be the preserve of the economically advanced.

Cultivating diverse datasets: In such a way, the AI algorithm does not present the risk of reproducing already existing biases. The variety of data employed in AI training has to be as diverse as the populations it services, cutting across several dimensions: race, gender, socioeconomic status, and learning abilities, to mention just a few.

Safeguarding Privacy and Data Integrity

These data-intensive AI systems, therefore, bring essential issues concerning privacy, especially on how information relating to students is collected, used, and safeguarded. These, thus, require from the educational institution and developers of the AI:

Implement Rob Protection Measures: Comjson Pvt. Ltd will comply with the highest standards for implementing security measures related to data, ensuring protection from unauthorised access and maintaining students' information in private confidence.

Ensure Transparency with Consent: Ensure transparency in data collection and use against students and parents by securing and obtaining informed consent while respecting an individual's right to privacy and control over personal information.

Embedding Ethical Considerations in AI Development

"Development and deployment of AI in education that ethical principles must guide; it has to be student-centred and ensure all-round development." This means:

AI Development Framework for Ethics: Developing detailed frameworks to ensure the implementation of ethical considerations in AI algorithms in the educational context, such as fairness, accountability, and transparency.

Inclusive development processes: Ejsons' EIGs will involve educators, students, and other Stakeholders in the development of AI to ensure that respective technologies are responsive to educational needs and ethical standards.

Promoting Digital Literacy and AI Fluency

Understanding AI and digital technologies is crucial to many things in this modern world. Thus, there is an unwavering social responsibility from educational institutions to:

Develop Digital Literacy as a Cross-Cutting Theme in Curricula: The cross-cutting curriculum is expected to prepare students for the adequate and proper use of digital tools and AI technologies, considering these elements with a critical understanding of all their potential and limits.

AI training for teachers: Involves using AI tools within their teaching domain, providing a way to effectively facilitate and transform the classroom while maintaining integrity in instruction and ethics towards AI.

Fostering Public Dialogue and Policy Development
Therefore, the strong impact of AI in education prompts the need for public dialogue and the development of comprehensive Policies that help the educational sector solve the ethical, social, and technical challenges that the integration of AI presents. These are:

Engage the community: Discussions should be carried out between educators, parents, students, and policy-makers on the appropriate application of AI within education to have a shared vision and agree on using AI openly, ethically, and responsibly.

Craft forward-looking policies: Policymakers should take the lead in crafting policies that will predict the development of AI so that the educational sector regulates and is at par with the technological upsurge while observing ethics and social responsibility.

The use of AI in education is an opportunity to improve the extent of learning experiences unheard of. But this promise would require a deep commitment to social responsibility, including ensuring equity, privacy protection, standards of ethics, digital literacy, and public dialogue. Working in these critical areas can give an orientation to the AI revolution: outcomes which are not just innovative but also lead to a narrowing focus of something less inclusive, ethical, and narrow compared to the more significant aims of education.

Creating Inclusive Educational Environments with AI

This further implies that artificial intelligence (AI) in the educational system advances the current systems towards real all-inclusive learning. Such an evolution would thus involve multi-dimensional approaches to technological innovation and strategic planning from an ethical perspective towards broad-based collaboration. Further exploration of the mechanisms and methodologies to use AI inclusively would provide insights into its transformative potential and the hurdles that must be dealt with.

Advanced Personalized Learning through AI

AI's power to tailor educational experiences to individual learners presents unparalleled opportunities for inclusion. Analysing information about students' learning habits can produce individualised learning modules that would make education available and efficient to every student, even those with learning disabilities or other problems not adequately addressed by standard methods.

Real-time adaptation dynamically allows learning paths to be modified for immediate support or challenge. It is a handy tool for students who are behind or need to accelerate content.

Multimodal Content Delivery: AI, by virtue, can provide knowledge in multiple forms: text, audio, video, or even interactive simulations and demonstrations. In this way, it will thus be able to address the varied nature of learning and the requirements of students who prefer learning through reading or listening, even attending to students living with physical disabilities.

Bridging the Access Gap

The promise of AI's democratising potential in education is contingent upon addressing the digital divide first. This is the only way to enable most students to access technologies that can equally transform their lives.

Mobile learning: AI-enabled educational apps are developed to work on mobile devices like smartphones, bringing the opportunity to learn to regions where personal computers are used less than smartphones.

Community involvement: Sharing resources may also be initiated through local participation and organisational collaboration when AI-based learning centres are established for students unable to study without technology at home.

Inclusive AI Development Processes
It depends on the AI tool's design to develop the AI tool with a philosophy that includes diversity and being actively involved in inclining biases towards harmfulness.

Ethical AI Development Frameworks: This is an approach to adopting a framework focused on transparency, accountability, and inclusivity from inception while developing AI.

Participatory Design involves a development process involving students, teachers, and other stakeholders so that the AI tools can be designed by understanding the diversity of needs of the end users.

Comprehensive Stakeholder Collaboration
AI has been seen to go beyond classroom borders and reach teachers, parents, policymakers, and even the general public since its current ability allows it to create even more inclusive educational environments.

Teacher Empowerment: Beyond the training previously acquired, there is a need for continuous support that would enable teachers to adjust to AI tools in teaching, which should include professional learning communities and technical support. Hence, they feel encouraged and confident in integrating AI into their practice.

Parental and Community Involvement: Orienting the parents and the community to the benefits and challenges of using AI in education creates a conducive environment with full support from all those involved in the learning process.

Ethical Considerations and Privacy Safeguards

However, the use of AI in education is often marked by critical ethical and privacy concerns, considering the safeguarding of students' rights.

Transparent data use: Communicate with the students and parents on how the data about them is used, stored, and kept to be accountable and gain trust.

Student-Centric Design: AI tools should be designed to improve education outcomes but not compromise the learners' autonomy or well-being. Thus, they should avoid designs subjecting the learners to more monitoring or pressure.

Implementation Challenges and Solutions

This paper provides a comprehensive view of the challenges to including AI in an educational setting, from technical barriers to ethical dilemmas. A practical solution must be found to these.

This interdisciplinary research will combine expert power from education, technology, psychology, and ethics to study the development of AI tools within sound pedagogy and responsible ethics.

Policy Innovation: Develop and implement policies supporting the ethical use of AI in education, guaranteeing its equal access to technology and protecting student privacy and data security.

Ongoing Evaluation: Design and develop mechanisms for evaluating AI tools in an education setting that may ascertain, on an ongoing basis, their preparedness to provide efficacy, inclusiveness, and responsiveness to all students.

Creating inclusive educational environments with AI represents a complex but profoundly impactful endeavour. We must work together to unlock AI's potential for personalised learning, address inequity in access, promote diversity of perspective on development, ensure ethical use, and secure the privacy and protection of users.

They assert that AI can centrally be instrumental in designing an education system that will respond to the necessities and longings for learning of every student, making it possible for them to realise their potential and play productive roles in an increasingly mediated world enabled by digital technology. That is through strategic setting up, collaboration, and commitment to equity and inclusion.

Ethical, Explainable and Responsible AGI in Education

This is where the concepts of Ethical, Explainable, and Responsible Artificial General Intelligence (AGI) become increasingly prominent in educational technology for the new age. AGI applied to the academic sphere may change the educational process of providing every student with personal learning experiences, automating administrative work, and providing information on learning patterns and outcomes, i.e., improving the efficiency of educational processes. However, deploying AGI in educational settings poses significant ethical, transparency, and responsibility concerns.

The Ethics of AI in Education in General

Introducing artificial intelligence (AI) in the educational sector would be revolutionary because it fosters personalised learning, perfectly managed administrative operations, and democratises access to quality education. However, the integration cannot be owed to some ethical quandaries. Thus, AI in education would require careful consideration of these four aspects: fairness, privacy, transparency, and lack of bias so that the technology will contribute ethically toward the educational environment.

The primary dominating ethical consideration remains the high level of assurance for fairness and accessibility. AI-based educational tools should be designed to meet the respective student's diversity so that even accessibility to the learning resources is ensured. On the other hand, if AI technologies are mainly available to institutions with ample resources, such as the very high-flying research-intensive universities, and it leaves the less-endowed schools behind, then it could work to the detriment of levelling the playing field in education. The key will be to devise strategies that ensure evenness in the diffusion of access to these innovations by all and sundry.

Issues of privacy: Most of the time, AI in education targets the capturing and analysing of gigantic volumes of students' data to customise learning experiences or enhance educational outcomes. There is room for significant privacy concerns, which must be exercised through strict observation of data protection measures. The data collection should occur in an open-transparent way between the school and technology provider, ensuring responsibility and, most importantly, safekeeping from unauthorised access; in this way, students and parents should be informed and aware, giving consent to participate.

Bias and Discrimination: AI systems are as unbiased as the data from which they were taught. The historical biases in this educational data could potentially yield discriminatory results if used to train AI models. For instance, admissions AI tools and grading systems may replicate unconscious prejudices favouring some demographic groups. Therefore, the treatment for this is critically warranting, ensuring, and dynamically monitoring the occurrence of biases in AI systems and taking necessary mitigation steps.

Transparency and accountability: AI systems' decision-making processes are complex and often somewhat opaque, far from being explainable in detail to the last instance, which might be required in decisions about learning paths or student assessment. This would mean establishing transparency in implementing AI tools in education to build student, educator, and parent trust. Clear accountability measures should be implemented when AI systems fail or result in damage.

Multi-pronged means that the whole approach to the ethical deployment of AI in education includes developing ethical guidelines, constantly ensuring fairness and bias, taking severe measures for data protection, and transparent communication to all parties. Those are the moral considerations that are addressed. This makes using AI to guarantee equity and inclusion possible while fully adhering to the individual's rights.

Ethical Considerations in AGI for Education

If such revolutionary systems as Artificial General Intelligence (AGI) came, which understand, learn, and apply knowledge to a larger scale of tasks at the same or superior level of competence to humans, their potential in the educational sector is nothing less than revolutionary.

However, bringing AGI into the processes of education is a very complex system of ethical issues that needs to be solved to make the most of its benefits while, on the other hand, avoiding possible harm. This includes ethical considerations for ensuring fairness and non-discrimination, privacy, mitigating biases, transparency and accountability, and broader consideration of sociotechnical impacts.

Accordingly, most ethical debates on AGI in education focus on privacy, data protection, and potential AGI bias. Since AGI systems could potentially involve processing and learning from large and diverse data sets, they might reasonably require processing sensitive information on students' learning habits, performance, and personal characteristics. It is part and parcel of preserving the trust of educational institutions to ensure that such data is protected and used appropriately.

Moreover, AGI systems need to be designed so that different kinds of biases can spoil their neutrality in providing recommendations or evaluations, and each student can have an equal chance for learning and further development. So, in education, ethical AGI deployment can take place without degrading the role of educators. Still, it will be able to bring to life the goal of improved human interaction and support rather than replacing human initiative.

Equitable Access and Fairness: The main concern of AGI from an educationally ethical perspective is ensuring equal access to such technologies. Due to this, AGI-powered education tools might present a risk of educational inequality only being accessible to institutions or learners possessing some resources, thus aggravating the existing educational inequalities. Efforts should be made so that AGI technologies and their development and deployment are accessible to all learners, irrespective of whether they belong to marginal or disadvantaged sections of society. These systems should also be designed to include different learning styles and needs to reflect fairness in education opportunities and results.

Protection of Privacy and Data: AI in education often involves collecting, analysing, and storing sensitive personal data on students. This raises enormous questions about privacy, whereby only AGI, with powerful data protection mechanisms, have to be guaranteed against access and misuse by unauthorised people. All their workings should be transparent in data collection, processing, and storage practices while seeking informed consent from the students or their guardians.

Bias and Discrimination: One of the ethical concerns with AGI is that the system would carry on with, if not worse, further the biases already in existence. This leads to discrimination because the AGI system originates in already existing data and thus inherits biases from the said data. One of the most critical aspects is recognising, mitigating, and monitoring the biases in AGI systems that can bring unfairness or discrimination against one group of students.

Transparency and Accountability: AGI decision-making can be so complicated that human beings cannot trace their decisions. This opacity could undermine trust in AGI systems, which is the most dangerous as soon as these are used for making or influencing big educational choices. It also assures enough transparency to let stakeholders understand how AGI systems work and make decisions. Adequate accountability mechanisms, including redress for harm, must also be stipulated where AGI systems fail to generate favourable outcomes.

Societal Effects and Impacts on the Student-Teacher Relationship: Introducing AGI to education can significantly contribute to socio-structures, and the student-teacher relationship can see a significant change. The AGI may offer a level of learning personalisation that was not possible before. At the same time, it also bears the risks of depreciating human components of education, including social, emotional, and ethical development usually experienced through interaction with teachers and fellow students.

One should bear in mind that AGI would enhance and not take over these aspects and that it, in no way, makes the education imparted partial or incomplete regarding the full intellectual, social, and emotional development of the learner.

In sum, this paper clearly shows that AGI holds the potential for meaningful change in the educational landscape. The ethical mind field of managing these risks, which could extract this value, is done carefully and proactively.

Addressing these ethical considerations of equitable access, privacy, bias, transparency, accountability, and societal impact will allow stakeholders to work together toward an educational future where AGI acts for good by enhancing all learners' academic experience and outcomes.

Explainable AGI in Education Explainability is a critical issue in educational contexts because the faculty believes that every decision or recommendation should be presented in a way that can be understood. Teachers, students, and parents must understand how and why the AGI system has generated a particular output when that affects learning paths, assessment results, or forms of content delivery.

Explainable AGI will further increase user confidence and trust by making it easy for them to intervene in AGI-transparent processes and empowering stakeholders to make their decisions based on informed insights provided by AGI.

Responsible AGI Deployment in Education Responsible deployment of AGI in education means deploying only those systems that enhance the quality of educational outcomes without causing harm. This should especially guard against negative impacts, such as technological dependence, loss of social interactions, and sometimes the furtherance of educational inequalities by AGI-based education.

Responsible AGI should also involve giving educators the adequate support and training they require to integrate these technologies into effective, varied teaching practices capable of being used by all students while ensuring AGI is a tool to support personalised learning and does not become just one more one-size-fits-all solution.

Prioritising Human-Centric Values A human-centred approach would consider AGI in education to augment, not replace, human capabilities. This comprises the design of AGI systems that support learning environments through collaboration, encourage critical thinking, and stimulate creativity.

AGI may place human values and needs at the fore. At the same time, it allows opportunities for creating educational experiences that are more inclusive, more engaging, and more effective in preparing the students for the challenges and opportunities facing them in the future.

Future Perspectives Thus, further development of AGI in education must be accompanied by continuous discussions among educators, technologists, policymakers, and ethicists about the ethical, explainable, and responsible use of the technologies.

Both will set clear guidelines and frameworks for AGI deployment, ensuring that these powerful tools may benefit students and educators, gain learning outcomes, and safeguard ethical standards and human values.

Lastly, involvement in developing and implementing AGI systems with a wide range of stakeholders, including students and parents, will improve the quality of these systems. The potential for AGI to revolutionise education is fraught with severe ethical, explainability, and responsibility considerations.

Proactively addressing these concerns will bring AGI to fruition and hold enormous potential for reaching a power that can significantly benefit educational experiences: more personalised and effective, accessible and equitable, transparent, and aligned with human values.

The future of AGI in education is more exciting. Still, we, the AGI users and developers, must tread through this future in a way that benefits every learner.

CHAPTER 11

Future Directions for AI in Education

As such, the 21st-century navigational journey sharpens the conjunction of Artificial Intelligence (AI) with education, signalling more than ever the need for a transformational shift in the pedagogical landscape. AI has increasingly started to be implemented in educational environments, transforming traditional teaching and learning practices to more personalised, efficient, and open conditions. This book explores these potential advances and what this might mean for students, educators, and the larger educational ecosystem through the lens of AI in education.

Personalisation at Scale

One of AI's biggest promises in offering education is realising genuinely personalised learning experiences. It could do so by making AI review large data pools about individual learning styles, preferences, and advancement, offering tailor-made learning paths for every student. Such systems will likely become fine-tuned in the future by using sophisticated algorithms, which can calibrate content on a real-time basis concerning learner engagement, levels of comprehension, and feedback. This level of personalisation will aspire to optimise each student's learning potential, tending to his academic necessities and emotional and psychological well-being.

Expanding the Role of Augmented and Virtual Reality

Combined with AI, augmented Reality (AR) and Virtual Reality (VR) promise to experience the learning process like never before. The technologies are up to the extent of moving a student to ancient civilisations, far-off planets, and even inside the human body to make a lifetime's learning possible, which was never heard of. With the development of AI, AR, and VR software, they will be more interactive, allowing the student to experiment with each element within the virtual space in a mode suitable to their progress and curiosity. This will increase engagement and retention and democratise access to educational experiences beyond traditional classrooms' scope.

Automation and Efficiency

A fundamental problem is the administrative burden on educators and their institutions, which AI stands to tackle. This is just the beginning; future AI advances are expected to go well beyond grading and scheduling to include complex administrative tasks like generating personalised feedback, developing curriculum, and even predictive analytics that can predict students falling behind. This will rationalise the operations of education in the sense that educators will reduce their workload and, in the process, have them spend more time on high-impact teaching activities that involve direct engagement of the students.

Bridging the Accessibility Gap

AI may make it possible for the power to make learners' education achievable throughout the world, including students who might have disabilities or who are located in remote places. In this regard, the students stand a chance to get customised learning materials that will be instrumental in breaking language barriers through innovations in speech recognition, language translation, and adaptive learning technologies, and also be able to adapt resources to its use in offering services to learners who are having an array of learning disabilities or learning preferences. This inclusivity is imperative in breaking down the educational barrier worldwide and providing quality education to people worldwide, irrespective of geography, economy, or the physical limit that may bar them from attending a traditional institutional educational centre.

The Ethical Dimension

As AI progressively grips the educational sector, the call to adhere to ethical guidelines becomes louder. Much more attention will need to be turned to data privacy, algorithmic bias, and the digital divide, which require more regulation and management in very different ways. The emphasis on maintaining trust and assurance of fairness in educational AI applications will be in the hands of these principles to ensure the AI system is transparent, equitable, and provides user privacy. Further development in the future will solely be based on the ethical use of AI to try and develop technologies for education that are inclusive, unbiased, and safe.

Preparing for an AI-Integrated Future

The successful integration of AI in education will need a shared partnership between educators, policymakers, and technologists. Educators will need to equip themselves with new teaching tools and methodologies. At the same time, policymakers will have to design frameworks for the ethical use of AI that will also address the digital divide. It will, therefore, be upon the technologist to ensure that the developed AI systems are advanced yet accessible and friendly to both the educator and student.

The future direction AI in education also points towards is a landscape in which learning becomes deeply personal, immersive and boundless experiences, and educational opportunities truly become accessible to all. Realising such a future will take carefully navigating the shoals of ethics and equity. But this AI keeps evolving: it has the potential to augment and even possibly revolutionise educational practice to a point whereby ways of

Engaging, inclusive, and practical education for all learners of the world could be possible.

Emerging AI Technologies and Their Potential Impact

The education domain is on the verge of being transformed by the fast changes in Artificial Intelligence (AI). This research will include brief presentations on the leading frontiers of AI advancements and how these could revolutionise education. Emerging AI technologies are set to redefine the educational space in terms of personalisation and engagement efficiencies with no historical precedent.

Natural Language Processing (NLP)

In such fast-changing technology and education canvases, the entry of Natural Language Processing (NLP) comes as a revolutionary force—one altering how learning is imparted and absorbed instead. This book focuses on NLP's broad impact on the educational sector. It seeks to bring out the applications and benefits of profound changes introduced into the industry by NLP. A careful understanding at the undergraduate level of the nuances of NLP may throw up valuable insights in the days ahead for education, bringing into sharp relief the synergy of artificial intelligence with the human learning process.

The Genesis of NLP in Education

Natural Language Processing (NLP) is a subdivision of artificial intelligence (AI) and scientific areas. In education, language inclusion marks quite a significant change, more so in closing the gap between computational systems and human linguistic abilities. Grading systems and learning experiences tailored specifically for the student are paradigms NLP has even begun to redefine, which education operates on to make learning more accessible, effective, and engaging.

Enhancing Personalised Learning

One of the most significant effects of NLP on education is individualising learning experiences. NLP examines the student's response, learning pace, and preferences to create an individual lesson plan and material. This refers to individualised learning styles and compensates for areas of deficit, allowing the learner's involvement and outcomes to be more effective.

Facilitating Automated Assessment

The assessment process has also seen an NLP impact revolution. Currently, the assessment methods used are NLP-based automated grading systems, which grade an open-ended response, essay, or even complex assignments in real-time by presenting feedback to the student. This reduces the educator's workload and provides a more objective method for this work. This allows for continuous assessment, and an educator can follow up on the learning progress more efficiently, thus intervening at any juncture deemed necessary.

Breaking Language Barriers

NLP has played a vital role in breaking language barriers in education. Translation language applications and tools helped open educational content for people whose first language is not theirs, thus democratising knowledge. Furthermore, through NLP-powered programs, one can learn languages by being provided with personal feedback and a better understanding of how the foreign language is spoken and grammatically articulated.

Enhancing Interactive Learning

NLP-powered interactive learning platforms are introducing a whole new dimension to education. Students can participate in interactive learning sessions with conversational agents and chatbots to answer questions, explain answers, and even have simulated discussion threads. This makes learning livelier, allowing instant clarification of doubts and sound delivery of the learning material.

Challenges and Ethical Considerations

Although NLP has its advantages, integrating it within education has its challenges: the possible risk of infringing data privacy, the concern of a digital divide, and having algorithms that display bias. These are the critical issues of the successful implementation of NLP tools in education: the accessibility of the presented tools to representatives of a given social class and their objectivity to the most significant possible degree.

The difference Natural Language Processing is likely to make in education may change the whole education scenario by facilitating individualistic learning opportunities, automated assessment mechanisms, breaking language barriers, and improved interactive learning. To unlock all the associated and moral benefits, overcoming all the related challenges and many ethical concerns is a must. The above capabilities of NLP are apparent and will have a considerable influence in shaping the future of learning as an integrated part of educational systems.

Machine Learning and Predictive Analytics

Technologies integrated with the education sector, such as Machine Learning (ML) and Predictive Analytics, will open new vistas of data-driven decision-making and provide a personalised learning experience. This essay talks about these technologies vis-à-vis how they are to revolutionise educational landscapes, help achieve better student outcomes, and make predictions regarding learning trends in the coming time. By allowing educators and institutions to make informed decision outcomes tailored to educational content and being proactive about students' needs, ML and predictive analytics do so by analysing patterns within massive datasets.

The Synergy of ML and Predictive Analytics in Education

Machine learning is a subfield of artificial intelligence that concentrates on giving algorithms to computers that make them learn from data and then allow the computers to make predictions or decisions from the data. On the contrary, predictive analytics uses statistics and data modelling techniques to determine future outcomes. These technologies all working together are creating unparalleled opportunities in education—from the possibility of custom learning paths to the early identification of at-risk students.

Personalised Learning Experiences

Some of the paramount uses of ML and Predictive Analytics in education include generating personalised learning experiences. The technologies seek to customise educational content, pacing, and learning strategies concerning individual students as per analysis conducted about their learning patterns, preferences, and performances. This becomes personalised to ensure that one gets more involved learners and improved support reflecting the strengths and areas of weakness that are being worked on, significantly improving outcomes.

Early Identification and Support for At-Risk Students

Identifying students at risk of underperforming or dropping out is a vital role of ML and predictive analytics. The process involves analysing data points that include issues related to attendance, grade books, and levels of engagement, which is critical in empowering educators by intervening much earlier and providing additional support and resources to them. This proactive approach helps mitigate challenges before they escalate, ensuring that all students can succeed.

Streamlining Administrative Tasks

ML and Predictive Analytics ease administrative burdens on educational institutions outside the classroom. More importantly, the space is no longer confined to just the four walls of a school. Still, ML and predictive analytics are disrupting institutions, from automated grading to admissions processes, through technologies that can take on all the mundane, repetitive tasks that educators and administrators waste time on. Furthermore, predictive models can assist in resource allocation, ensuring that schools operate optimally.

Enhancing Curriculum Development and Instructional Strategies

It has a significant impact on the curriculum and development of the instructional strategy. Educators can adjust and improve teaching methods and materials if they know what content works and is complex for the learners. This data-driven approach ensures that curricula are relevant, engaging, and effective in meeting educational goals.

Challenges and Considerations

Of course, applying ML and Predictive Analytics in education, like in any other industry, is not challenge-free. Issues on data privacy, security, and ethical use abound. The integrity of educational institutions is grounded in the responsible protection and use of student data. This then calls for the continued rigorous evaluation of the technologies to avoid biases in their contribution, or even detrimental, to realising educational equity.

Introducing Machine Learning (ML) and Predictive Analytics in the educational sector proved game-changers, inviting insights and innovations that were not even thinkable earlier.

However, this induction is open to challenges. This book discusses the complexities and challenges of applying ML and predictive analytics in education, supported by cases of ethical issues on data privacy, equity, and the digital divide. This insight into the challenges is put in place to give stakeholders a better arena to move up and about these stumbling blocks and ensure that such technologies are enablers but do not become complicators of the educational landscape.

Ethical Considerations

Ethical considerations are among the challenges of using ML and predictive analytics in education. Much concern arises from what data is collected, how it is collected, how the same data is being used and by whom this data is accessible. For instance, if not well-designed and guided, predictive models may be used to introduce biases indirectly.

Therefore, applying these technologies should involve an ethical responsibility to be employed reasonably, transparently, and accountably since the consequences of misuse have long-term effects on the students' lives.

Data Privacy and Security

The question of data privacy and security falls under ethical considerations. Universities are custodians of a vast amount of sensitive information. Using ML and Predictive Analytics includes data collection, analyses, and storage, which may be a reason for breaches and unauthorised access. Security must be severe, ensuring that access to student data is guaranteed with confidentiality and integrity.

The Digital Divide

The other crucial challenge which directly opposes the equitable use of ML and predictive analytics in education is the "digital divide." Institutions must be revised to access the technology and infrastructure required to support the advanced analytical toolset.

This may further increase the education gap, whereby students from under-resourced schools are not benefiting from the technologies' personalised learning and early intervention tools.

Bias and Fairness

Another salient challenge that has received much more attention is the bias in ML models and the fairness of predictive analytics. ML algorithms likely quickly pick up and propagate the data they learn from societal biases efficiently.

This may give rise to unfair predictions and decisions, affecting the educational opportunities and outcomes of the students. Ensuring fairness, therefore, can be an endeavour of continuous efforts in model design and implementation, monitoring to ensure the implemented algorithms do not have biased assertions.

Implementation and Integration Challenges

Integrating ML and predictive analytics into implementing the existing educational framework poses pragmatic challenges. These might involve issues such as teachers and administrators needing better skills to use the technologies effectively.

Integrating such innovations with new technology in the curriculum is highly time-consuming and requires scarce resources in most educational settings. Comprehensive professional development for educators can only overcome this barrier.

The Challenge of Interpretability and Accountability

"Black box" is a term often used for ML and Predictions in predictive analytics, in which human decisions are made in ways humans don't readily understand. So, for educational contexts, where reason is essential to understanding the "way things have been done," lack of interpretability could be a real problem.

Accountability in using these technologies means devising accurate, interpretable, transparent models to ensure interpretability.

The challenges to including Machine Learning and Predictive Analytics in education are massive: ethical, privacy, equity, bias, implementation, and interpretability problems. This would mean an enormous effort from politicians, educators, technologists, and the community.

Fully harnessed the potential of ML and Predictive Analytics through ethical use, data privacy, and security with the aim of digital divide, fairness, and support to educators through training and resources.

But whatever their path, one aspiration is clear: the concept of being able to use powerful technologies in a way that furthers, strengthens, and deepens educational outcomes for all students, making learning more personalised, engaging, and effective.

Machine learning and predictive analytics are altering the landscape in education by developing cutting-edge solutions for some of the most age-old problems.

Further, this technology can substantially enhance learning results through assistance in personalised learning experiences, student risk identification, and at-risk student support, thereby improving administrative processes and curriculum.

However, their successful integration requires careful consideration of ethical, privacy, and security concerns. In the future, how the application of ML and predictive analytics proceeds thoughtfully in education will hold critical perspectives to shape the future of learning—education will become much more accessible, efficient, and effective for all.

Navigating the Future: AI Challenges in Education and Strategies for Success

Education with Artificial Intelligence (AI) integration will bring innovations and opportunities but will also have formidable challenges for educators, policymakers, and technologists. This paper will outline the most critical challenges faced by the educational sector by AI and recommend ways to handle them appropriately.

Besides ensuring AI is human-complementary in teaching, ethical considerations, equity, access, data privacy, and teacher and student preparedness are all important to our leveraged possibilities in AI for improved educational outcomes and must be adhered to strictly.

Ethical Considerations in AI Implementation

One of AI's most significant challenges to education and learning is guaranteeing an ethical use of the technology within those systems. Therefore, AI technology should be able to contribute to advancing educational needs that respect the dignity and rights of the learners. There always remains a danger that it is used to shore up extant inequities or introduce new biases.

Navigation Strategy: Clearly outline the ethical guidelines and standards for using AI in education. Show how they will develop the AI systems, including regular auditing of the AI systems for bias and engaging diverse stakeholders in developing AI that would serve the broad educational community equitably.

Equity and Access to AI Resources

The genuine concern is the digital divide on an implementation basis. Only some students will have access to the level of technology and connectivity required to practice AI-related learning concepts.

Navigation Strategy: Building a bridge with the Digital Divide would take focused investment in infrastructure, emphasising schools and communities that are least resourced. Providing devices and ensuring access to the Internet, including offering an AI literacy program for its progress, could show that all students were involved.

Data Privacy and Security

The enormous datasets the AI systems use raise concerns about the privacy and security of sensitive educational information. In this regard, misusing students' data would have far-reaching consequences for student privacy and academic paths.

Navigation strategy: Therefore, when developing laws and regulations to guard the security of AI systems, educational technologists concerned with AI systems' security will always prioritise rules and regulations such as the Family Educational Rights and Privacy Act (FERPA) in the USA. Transparency with students and parents about how data is used and safeguarded is also vital.

Preparing Teachers and Students for an AI-Enhanced Future

This would require preparing teachers and students for the infusion of AI in the educational process, which includes pedagogical uses and critical reflection on AI's societal implications.

Navigation Strategy: AI literacy should be part of the professional development of teachers and curriculum development at each stage. They must develop deep knowledge and skills to integrate AI tools into teaching methods. Similarly, students also need to learn digital literacy and be able to attain it.

Ensuring AI Complements Human Teaching

However, ensuring that AI adds value rather than replaces human teaching is a huge challenge. The value that a human educator adds through empathy, understanding, and moral guidance is invaluable.

Navigation AI Strategy: AI should be designed and implemented to support and enhance the teacher's role but does not substitute for it. This usage could involve the use of AI not only in administrative but also in analytics assignments, which would give the teachers enough space and time to pay due attention to their student's social, emotional, and cognitive development.

The path forward in integrating AI into education is fraught with challenges but also ripe with opportunity. Ethical considerations, equity and access, and data privacy concerns will have to be addressed, all pointing towards the successful use of such high-end technologies in education.

We may strive to ensure a set of proper ethical considerations and business with AI to aid educational processes without replacing them. The point is to avoid getting mixed with AI in education.

Still, the fact is that the education experience should be better for all students, providing an equal level playing field for inclusiveness, innovation, and lifelong learning.

As this new era moves forward, educators, policymakers, technologists, and the community will collaborate to ensure the fructification of AI's full potential in education.

Vision for a Globally Connected AI-Enhanced Education System

Following the 21st century, education experienced a sharp change. Significant artificial intelligence (AI) improvements occurred, and the world became more interrelated. Today's technologies offer a lifetime opportunity to customise a learning experience according to individual requirements, potentially permeating geographical boundaries and educational disparities.

This book conceives of an education system intertwined with the world and supported by AI, which reboots the methodologies of both learning and teaching using technology to make quality education available to one and all. Keeping this in mind, let us look at some possible benefits and challenges an AI-integrated education system would offer and the areas of action that must be imagined for this grand vision to become a reality.

The Current State of Global Education

However, the gaps still need to be addressed despite great global strides in educational access. Millions of children and millions of adults, in turn, continue to be denied the fundamental basic skills of learning and numeracy. The quality of education differs significantly among regions.

Already, technology has started influencing education, as the development of digital platforms and digital learning resources is underway. Nevertheless, incorporating such is quite uneven, even deepening the gap of advantages between the most and the least advantaged.

These disparities were brought to the forefront and widened through the COVID-19 pandemic, simultaneously showing technology's possible and impossible abilities in education. A transition towards a more equitable, effective educational model is needed to address these challenges head-on.

The following section reveals how AI and worldwide connectivity may address persistent challenges that are resistant to change and, in fact, really alter the education landscape. The part to follow delves into the role of AI in education, current applications, and future possibilities.

The Role of Artificial Intelligence in Education

With great promises to improve learning outcomes and teaching efficiency, artificial intelligence (AI) is increasingly taking an oppressive force in transforming the face of education. Currently, some of the areas in education that AI has been applied to include:

Personalisation: Algorithms of artificial intelligence help analyse individual patterns of learning and then make it suitable for each student through providing content that provides for their learning pace and style. This serves for customisation, identifying the strengths and weaknesses so that the needed support can be ascertained precisely where students need it.

Automated Grading and Feedback: It is also a modern possibility to use AI systems for grading assignments. These systems can grade assignments and give necessary feedback to students, saving teachers time and allowing them to pay more attention to teaching instead of improving administrative skills.

Interactive Learning Environments: AI enforces and strengthens educational software and games to make learning easy, fun, and interactive for pupils.

Prediction Analytics: With AI, it becomes possible to predict student performance and likely outcomes. In cases where students risk falling through or not fulfilling their potential, this will be brought out for an early intervention period.

The potential for AI in the education sector is very huge. It promises a revolutionised way through which the efficiency of processes can be improved and changed through learning. Educators would be able to offer, with the help of AI, a more inclusive, equally practical education.

Vision for a Globally Connected AI-enhanced Education System

• *Vision:* an audacious, bold world that shall enable leveraging technology in this ever-interconnected universe to craft an AI-hastened education system and guarantee a more inclusive educational ecosystem for all persons worldwide. Here's a vision of what that could look like:

• *Global Connectivity:* The prime of the worldwide connectivity core of this vision is enabling sharing across borders of developed best practices, knowledge, and educational resources. This will ensure a community of global learners and educators by making available high-quality educational resources for everybody.

• *AI integration:* The AI should adapt to different education needs worldwide. This would mean having systems adaptable to any language, culture, and, most importantly, academic standards, thus giving personalised learning to each student, even those learning from remote locations and their background history.

• *Personalized Learning:* AI has the potential to offer students a personalised education program solely dependent on their learning progress. This way, learning is accelerated, and students stay motivated since the learning pace is more accessible, enjoyable, and relevant to their needs and interests.

• *Teacher empowerment:* The tools will also help reduce administrative burden, provide insights into how some things are progressing with students, and even recommend interventions suited to individual students for the teacher. This will further empower teachers to engage more in creative and critical teaching methods, leading to a dynamic and interactive classroom.

• *Accessibility and inclusiveness:* The system has to be thrown open to ensure all types of inclusiveness from one and all across different geographical divides. This all-inclusiveness should include making the technology affordable and user-friendly, creating content concerning cultural diversities, and training educators to use the AI tools effectively.

Challenges and Considerations

As glamorous as it sounds to envisage a world-linked, AI-backed education system, the road to that future is paved with several hurdles and issues.

Ethical consideration: AI in education raises critical questions of privacy, data security, and risks of algorithmic bias with probabilistic outcomes. Only transparent, safe, and fair AI systems will gain trust in the minds of students, educators, and parents as service users of education.

• *Technological Disparities:* This is a significant barrier to technology. This calls for investment in infrastructure, while educational content and AI technologies must be adaptable to low-resource settings.

• *Cultural Sensitivity:* The system should respect the cultural sensitivity of educational contents and algorithms for AI to be developed, hence involving and respecting the diversities of the global student community.

• *Sustainability:* This area will focus on economic and environmental sustainability while developing and maintaining a globally connected, AI-infused education system. It will involve the technology used and its implications for cost and environment.

Steps Towards Realisation

Realising a globally connected and AI-boosted education system will require multifaceted approaches, including policy development, technological innovation, and broad-based cooperation among the stakeholders.

Further, it should be mentioned three more essential directions that are to be paid attention to, bringing this vision closer to realisation:

• ***Develop support policy:*** The government and international bodies should develop policies supporting AI integration in education. This will include research funding and development, setting data privacy standards and ethical AI use, and creating protection frameworks that support innovation while protecting students and educators.

• ***Public-Private Partnerships:*** Contributions from the public and private sectors, including firms and non-profits, would foster developing and deploying AI-based technologies in education.

The partnership would constitute the integrated ability of the three industries to provide efficient technological solutions, infrastructure, and financing that would connect the education system to the world.

• ***Infrastructure Development***: Investment in digital infrastructure is critical, especially in the most affected areas. This calls for internet access and issues with hardware and software that support such learning, including AI. Guaranteed reliable, broad access would play the most significant role in enabling an inclusive and effective system.

• ***Training and educators' support:*** The preparation of training teachers and educators, besides extending continuous support, is required so that they may make sensible use of the AI tools in the teaching-learning process.

Subsequently, professional development programs that work on technology integrated into the classroom and highlight AI as an enhancer of teachers' roles and not as a replacement also become necessary.

• ***Community Engagement:*** When the community, that is, the students, the parents, and local leadership, is involved in the design and even implementation of programs, the education system can guarantee that it can respond to its needs with respect for its value system. Feedback and participatory design mechanisms could facilitate further adaptations to different cultural contexts and educational systems.

• ***Continuous Evaluation and Adaptation:***
The full implementation of the globally connected, AI-enhanced education system is constant. There is a need for continued monitoring and evaluation of AI's influence on learning outcomes and education equity.

In other words, the vision of the AI-inclusive education system, which would be related to the world, represents a significant step toward enabling quality education accessible to everybody, suited for every learner's needs, and available irrespective of place and socioeconomic development.

This mission entails artificial intelligence working to empower educators with a more personalised, engaging, and inclusive learning experience that touches new levels of effectiveness.

Nonetheless, to realise the vision, considering the ethical, technological, and cultural challenges, governments, technology providers, educational institutions, and communities must collaborate.

By meeting these challenges head-on and moving proactively toward AI implementation, we must take advantage of the chance that this use affords us to transform education. In the eyes of the future, it is a path truly laden with promise for a globally connected and AI-enhanced education system.

This calls to action for everyone in the quest to shape a very inclusive, effective, and innovative educational landscape for future generations.

It will help build an education system that uses cutting-edge technology to benefit every learner, fulfilling the dream of quality education for all.

CHAPTER 12

How AI is Transforming Education Across the Globe

Artificial intelligence (AI) has become an emerging intervention in the education system worldwide, changing how teaching and learning methods are implemented. This review aims to synthesise critical findings and insights from recent research on the worldwide developments of AI in education.

Global Trends and Research Focus The countries that have shown much concentration include China, India, and the United States, which have taken to the forefront of AI research in education, following this field and social sciences, specifically in computer science and engineering.

An international organisation has initiated an initiative to encourage and develop AI's diverse applications, from online learning to distance education.

Revolutionary changes in education practices are now spearheaded by AI technologies such as natural language processing, machine learning, and adaptive learning systems, all of which promise a great leap forward in personalised and efficient learning.

AI has introduced natural language processing, machine learning, and adaptive learning systems that modify educational practices into more effective and

Challenges and Opportunities

However, specific privacy and ethical considerations exist for AI integration in education. To make AI full-fledged, these challenges must be addressed to improve personalised learning and operational efficiency with the help of tools like intelligent tutoring systems and automated grading.

Further, AI in education encompasses applications ranging from research trends to practical challenges witnessed over the last decade and is, therefore, a vividly evolving field.

Impact on Teaching and Learning

AI has been recognised for its capacity to enhance teaching and learning without replacing human educators. The unique human qualities, like critical thinking and creativity, make man different from other life forms.

This underscores the future of education when humans will work with AI. Besides, generative AI tools like ChatGPT are opening new doors for innovative teaching practices. Generative AI tools mainly affect education by producing human-like text, images, and interactive simulations.

Ethical and Responsible Use of AI Ethical considerations include fairness, accountability, transparency, and bias issues related to AI in education. The report points out the significance of community-based leadership in handling these ethical matters to ensure AI use in schooling is within the broader social values and principles.

In parallel, the development of such tools as the Transparency Index underscores transparency's salience in AI-powered educational technologies for the other ethical dimensions: interpretability and safety.

The Global Renaissance: AI's Transformation of Education

Integrating Artificial Intelligence (AI) in education opens doors for a world renaissance in shaping teaching and learning paradigms on all continents. The transformation speaks to the technological change and a more inclusive, personalised, and efficient global education system.

The impact of AI in education is multidimensional, ranging from student engagement to teacher effectiveness and global effects on educational equity. AI enables more of the world's diverse populations to access quality education.

Personalised Learning at Scale At its most fundamental level, AI will impact global education by enabling mass education to the differing individual needs of millions of learners from extremely varied geographic, socio-economic, and cultural backgrounds.

Most traditional education systems, which use a one-size-fits-all methodology, cannot accommodate students' different paces and learning needs.

It will simply break down those barriers, using data analysis to customise learning to a student's strengths, weaknesses, and preferences. This means that students' motivation and engagement will thus be very high, bringing better learning outcomes because it addresses each student's needs.

Educational platforms powered by such AI promise to fill the void of providing excellent quality, personalised education when the reach of quality educators is far and poor in vast rural populations, even in countries.

 For example, AI-powered learning apps exist in some parts of Africa and Asia. Their mission is to deliver quality education in a natural language that anyone can take.

The learning apps adapt content to the learner's proficiency level and provide feedback that guides the learner's learning journey.

This demonstrates how AI can make education available and attainable to many more people, enabling it to reach the global level of personalised learning.

Bridging Educational Gaps with Intelligent Tutoring Systems

Intelligent Tutoring Systems (ITS) portray the promise of AI in realising equitable educational opportunities worldwide. The ITS offers tailor-made instruction and feedback to a student in a way that represents a human tutor but benefits from the ability to scale even to a student residing in the most remote areas.

These areas, ITS promises, would be victims of proper and consistent education due to an acute shortage of qualified teachers.

Further, ITS platforms are increasingly multilingual since they serve students worldwide and help preserve local languages and cultures by incorporating such into the curriculum.

Such an international perspective enhances learning outcomes by fostering a sense of identity and community in learners from diverse backgrounds. Automating Administrative Tasks for Global Efficiency

And, to be sure, this is a universal problem: the volume of administrative work that falls on the shoulders of educational establishments takes away time and resources from teaching and learning. AI's ability to automate most tasks, from grading to taking attendance and scheduling, is all set to turn the world of education upside down.

This automation streamlines operations, reduces costs, and allows educators to focus on their primary mission: teaching. Therefore, these efficiency gains from AI would significantly impact many developing countries where educational resources are already scarce. For example, the financial resources that could be better available to schools could be utilised toward classroom instruction improvement and expanded access to education rather than locked up in administrative functions.

Overcoming Language Barriers Language diversity is a big challenge for the world in education, as most students are asked to speak a second language or dialect with which they are uncomfortable.

This, in turn, can break language barriers and make education accessible to each student in every corner of the world with the help of AI-powered language learning tools and real-time translation services. It is meant to help with language acquisition and make educational content available in many languages so that language variation will not hinder education.

AI is leading the worldwide revolution in education, with learning that is more personalised, accessible, and efficient.

What makes this component of this global education system inclusive and very influential is the individualised adaptation of education content to the needs of each learner, the scale of tutoring services, the automation of administrative services, and relief from the language barrier.

AI is likely to span these educational divides in the coming years as it unfolds to assimilate with global educational frameworks, thus ensuring quality education to students, irrespective of their geographical and socioeconomic status. This global renaissance in education, powered by AI, is not about technology but about unleashing human potential on an entirely new plane.

Future Directions

The future of AI in education involves much more innovation and even closer partnership between the AI system and human teachers.

This partnership aims to raise intelligence and decrease educators' workload by providing intelligent classroom orchestration, especially in language learning.

These include technologies such as ChatGPT and GPT-4, designed to enable personalised education and rapid feedback loops within the learning environment, even as scholars' challenges border on the effectiveness of the technologies and ethical considerations.

In brief, the current global scenario of AI use in education represents a turning point for the education sector, driven almost wholly by developments in AI technologies.

The ability to learn at an individual level, greater productivity, and innovation in teaching place the impetus for using AI firmly on the future of education. However, ethical, privacy and operational challenges must be dealt with in a befitting manner to derive the best possible benefits from using AI in educational setups worldwide.

EPILOGUE

Turning the last page in our exploration of Artificial Intelligence in Education, we stand on the brink of a new era. These pages have shown the complex tapestry of AI's role in transforming educational paradigms, unveiling its unequalled promise and the tricky ethical issues it throws down.

We have been to tomorrow's classrooms, filled with new AI-powered, personalised learning environments to match individual learners' unique needs and learning paces. The concept of one-size-fits-all education has been abolished, and now several learning styles and intelligence are valued in the system.

Our study took us to the core of AI-driven analytics and its influence on educational strategies. Because of data analytics, we could identify teaching gaps and differentiate simultaneously to build a more inclusive learning environment that does not seek to leave any student behind.

But this journey has also illuminated AI's shadowy ethical implications for education. We saw the pitfalls of data privacy, the digital divide, and AI's potential to carry forward its biases. All these challenges, therefore, point to our collective, conscientious efforts in navigating the ethical labyrinth so that AI becomes a force for equitable education.

As we close this chapter, it's clear that the dialogue between AI and education is only just beginning. AI's potential to revolutionise education is boundless, yet it demands a vigilant and nuanced approach.

This will call for an informed, concerted effort between policymakers, educators, technologists, and society to ensure the leveraging of AI in education for efficiency and personalisation, acting as a catalyst for inclusivity, creativity, and empowerment. It's like a canvas, the future of education—yet to be fully painted, and AI has the brush. It is for us to guide its hand so that every stroke delivered is one of those to compose a masterpiece of educational equity, innovation, and human flourishing.

So, let's move forward with optimism, grit, and an unshaken belief that, with responsible deployment and application of AI, the frontiers of what we know in learning, teaching, and growing can be pushed back.

About the Author

This book, **AI in Education**, is written in an accessible and non-technical style by Constantine Leo Serafim.

The author is a true pioneer in Computer Science, boasting an impressive career that spans over half a century.

His unparalleled expertise and dedication left an incredible mark on the public and private sectors.

Beyond his work on government and NGO projects, Serafim is also a prolific inventor known for his product designs for dementia patients.

Another published book by the same author is:

ARTIFICIAL INTELLIGENCE in Healthcare

A Non-Technical Look At The Future of Medicine